# The 9 C's
C C C C C C C
## To Career Confidence

**By Julie Leatherland**

**Your practical, interactive workbook in helping you determine what job, career or business is best for your personality.**

ISBN: 978-1-9998671-1-9

Published by Ann Jaloba Publishing, Sheffield S10 2QH

**Note to Readers**

# Table of Contents

## Dedications and thanks

I would like to dedicate this book to my husband Robin (Robbie) Timms. For without his endless love, support and this workbook would have just been a pipe dream. And if I hadn't written it, it would have been a big regret in later life. So, thanks Robbie for your endless love, support and backing in giving me the confidence in getting started and writing this workbook

I can't thank you enough for putting up with me typing into the early hours of the morning, and then putting my cold hands and feet on you when I eventually got into bed to warm them up (and very nice it was indeed). Thanks for listening endlessly about personality types, the best Aesop's Fables to put in, for answering endless questions and giving your opinion and points of view. For doing the shopping, cooking me my dinner and washing-up. And generally doing everything you could do to give me the much-needed time and space to write, while also working full-time in your own job.

So, thank you so much Robbie, I couldn't have done it without you.

> **"You just have to keep on doing what you do. It's the lesson I get from my husband; he just says: Keep going. Start by starting".**
> **Meryl Streep**

I would also like to thank Dr. Sue Peacock, Julie Futcher, Paul Simmons, and Jill Cassidy for their truly inspiring stories, which were written from the heart especially for this workbook. Thank you once again for taking the time and effort to write them for me.

Lastly, I would like to thank Ann Jaloba of Ann Jaloba Publishing for helping, guiding, and supporting me in getting this workbook from an idea on paper into a published book. Thank you, Ann, for everything you have done for me.

# About Julie the author and her workbook

Hello and thank you for buying this workbook.

My name is Julie Leatherland and my true passion is working both men and women just like you. That is people who want to make changes in their jobs, careers, or businesses, but are unsure how or where to start.

This workbook has been specially written to help build up your self-confidence and self-esteem beyond belief. To give you the courage, the drive, and the determination to get out there and do what you really want to do in life. To do that that thing that is based in honesty, realism, and practicality. That is going to make you feel happy, fulfilled, and alive once again.

So, how do you achieve this? By taking a good long hard look at yourself as a whole person, and not just a list of haves and have nots! To work through the chapters, do the required work, read the stories, and implement what you have learned by putting it into practice.

The workbook encompasses the physical, mental, emotional, and psychological aspects of yourselves, your personality type, alongside the practical and realistic stuff like skills, knowledge, and experience.

The men and women who have successfully used the workbook are:

- Are first starting out in the world of work, after leaving school, college, or university.
- Have just completed an apprenticeship, vocational work, or work experience.
- Are returning to work, after having children.
- Are returning to work, after a period of absence due to sickness or ill-health.
- Are returning to work after looking after / caring for someone else.
- Is facing redundancy or being laid-off.
- Have been made redundant.
- Wants a career change.

The main idea of the workbook is to help you look at the practical and realistic aspects of yourself and your personality, so that that you have the confidence to start looking for a job, career or business that is best suited to you, and your personality. This will give yourself the career edge, because it helps you to realistically recognise your own strengths and weaknesses alongside the skills, knowledge, and experiences you already possess. We will look at the individual quirks, idiosyncrasies and foibles that make you the truly unique and special person you are. And how you can bring all of this into the workplace, and to give you the career edge for your ideal job, career or business that suits you.

Whatever reason for you using this workbook, the biggest thing I have found over the years of doing career coaching, is that the career coaches who tend to be the most successful, are the ones who accept without a doubt that people have different personality types and character types that suit different jobs and work with their own personalities and characters to be the very best they can be to give them their career edge.

Repeatedly, I have worked with people who were not cut out for a certain profession or job type. And wondered why they were unhappy, miserable, anxious, and stressed, both at work and at home. But once they worked with me and found a job or career that realistically and practically suited them, their temperament, character, and nature, they found once again that inner peace, calm and tranquillity. They found going to work a pleasure, rather than a chore. Who would not want to have all that and more?

I think the Chinese philosopher Confucius sums it up quite eloquently here:

---

**"Choose a job you love,**
**and you will never have to work a day in your life".**
**Confucius**

---

So, how does the workbook work? We all have a stronger leaning to a certain personality type or profile. This is an integral part of us and who we are. What I have created especially for this workbook, are four different and distinct personality types for you to work with. I have named these: The White Dove, which is symbolised by the colour green. The Serene Swan, which is symbolised by the colour blue. The Ruling Rooster which is symbolised by the colour red and The Proud Peacock, which is symbolised by the colour yellow. We are a mixture of all four personality types, but with stronger leaning towards one, (the other two personality types are there as a support act, to give us balance). Within these four individual personality types we all exhibit certain traits, characteristics, attributes, and skills that suit certain jobs, careers, or businesses.

Understanding what your predominant personality type, will give you a distinct edge in looking at what job, career or business is best suited to you, and your personality type. The workbook is designed to help you recognise your own beliefs and thinking, and the way you view yourself and the world around you, and that has been holding you back from what you dream. This is achieved by taking a good look at you and your beliefs, the way you think, feel, act, and behave through specially designed interactive written exercises, reflection work, motivational quotes, inspirational stories, poems, and fables.

HOWEVER, this workbook is not a magic wand. And like anything in life, the more you put in – the more you will get out of it. So, if you put 100% in, then the workbook will help give you the ultimate in self-confidence, self-belief, and self-acceptance of who you are. What you can or cannot do, what you can achieve or cannot achieve. What you need to work on and what you need to do to get there.

So, who is this workbook suitable for? The workbook is suitable for anyone who wants a real and practical, down-to-earth, direct, no-nonsense approach at looking at themselves, their personalities and what makes them "tick". In a language and in a way that you will find easy to understand and to work with.

## More about Julie

I was born and raised in Northampton (UK) and lived there with my mum and late father and younger sister until I left home and went travelling in the mid 1980's. I returned back to Northampton in the early 1990's and have lived and worked here ever since, running my own business since 2007.

I am happily married to Robin (Robbie) and we both enjoy eating out, having a glass of red wine or two, watching films and canal walks.

My career background is as diverse as the people I have helped over the years. Since leaving school in 1982, I have done a wide range of jobs. From working in a Casino as a Croupier and Casino Inspector (Supervisor) for 10 years. And travelling all over the world doing it. To working as a Cashier and Regional Trainer for a well-known Catalogue Shop in the 1990s. To working as a British Telecoms (BT) 192 Telephone Operator, giving out telephone numbers and information to the public. To working for Trading Standards advising the public on what legal actions they can take if they had problems with their domestic or commercial energy suppliers. In 2000, I went back to working in casinos. But this time as a Branch HR/Administrator. And it was during this time that I was approached by GamCare (the gaming industries national organisation for people with gambling problems), to be a liaison between them and casinos to set up help and support for people with gambling problems. Unfortunately, I was made redundant before it came to fruition.

So, in 2006 I started to train part-time as a Hypnotherapist, NLP (Neuro Linguistics Programme) Practitioner, Counsellor and Psychotherapist.

And set up my own business after qualifying in 2007, whist still working part-time in the casino. I continued to study and gained a further qualification, an Advanced Diploma in Counselling and Psychotherapy in 2009.

In 2012 I started to study again and went more down the Coaching route, and utilised my skills, knowledge, and experience in combining both the therapeutic process with NLP and coaching. This works well in helping people move on forward by helping them to change the way they think, feel, act, and behave.

It is within this period of study that I developed a real interest in personality typing and personality traits. And saw the correlation between people's personality types and traits, and the jobs, careers, and businesses best suited to them. I particularly liked the Psycho-Analysis Personality typing methodology. And after further research, I found the Holland Codes Career Personality Typing. I professionally found that combining the two of them together alongside elements of NLP and Psychotherapy, was more of a dynamic way in looking at people's behaviours, beliefs, and attitudes, rather than the Myers-Briggs or DISK Assessment alone. And through trial and error, I have combined the two methodologies to create a truly personalised and unique way at looking at you, your personality and different aspects of a job, career, or business that you might not have seen the similarities, or a correlation of skills, attributes, or attitudes, that goes with a particular personality type or trait.

So, it is through my work with my past clients with Personality Typing and Career Assessment Coaching is where this workbook was born. This workbook is all about you looking, assessing, and making the most of your existing and newfound skills, knowledge, life experiences, personal and physical attributes. And combining it with your personality type and traits to create a personal template, in which you can realistically assess an ideal job, career or business, that is going to suit you, and the way that you think, feel and act.

My job is to help facilitate this through a well-organised, structured, and highly interactive, client-led programme, that is done on a one-to-one basis. Or you can choose to go through the programme yourself. Everything you need is contained within the workbook.

I genuinely hope you enjoy doing it, as much as I enjoyed writing and researching for it.

> ## "I once went job hunting and hired myself. I have never looked back".
>
> ## Anonymous

**Inspiration Time**

Below is an inspiration piece written by Dr. Sue Peacock titled – From past to present. This piece reflects her hard work, determination, motivation, and positive thinking, that has gotten her where she is today. At the top of her game in the NHS, she took the plunge to leave and to set up her own self-employed business as a Therapist/Psychologist in 2017.

Upon leaving school, I was determined to be a physiotherapist and had arranged to work as a physiotherapy assistant prior to going to University. I hadn't even considered psychology as an option. This turned out to be a good move having failed my A levels, I would not have gotten a place anyway! So, whilst working full time as a physiotherapy assistant, I studied different A levels at night school and passed! My experience working in the physiotherapy department was invaluable, in that it taught me about the politics of the NHS, but more importantly it taught me important people skills such as respecting dignity and showing compassion.

One of my more tedious tasks turned out to be a turning point in my life. This task involved sorting out the referrals for out-patient physiotherapy, and I noticed that the same names kept appearing every few months, and I wondered why these people kept coming back and what could we do to help them, so they wouldn't keep returning and I realised these people had chronic pain. I read a little around chronic pain and at this point decided that psychology was going to be the career for me working with people who have chronic pain.

Whilst studying for my initial psychology degree, I contacted a local psychologist who was running pain management programmes and I worked as a volunteer helping her to run them. This eventually lead to paid assistant psychologist work. Whilst studying for my MSc in Health Psychology, I had to return to my physiotherapy assistant post to pay for my course fees. I used this opportunity to write my thesis on relaxation as a treatment for phantom limb pain, as part of my job at that time was running the amputee rehabilitation group. From there I moved into health promotion and was involved in a variety of projects such as sexual health and workplace health promotion. At the onset of smoking cessation services, I was asked to set up the service from scratch in the Luton Health Action Zone, which was successful and became a countywide service for Luton and Bedfordshire.

Meanwhile, whilst working in health promotion, I was offered the opportunity to work in the pain clinic at Milton Keynes Hospital to set up and develop pain management programmes. Initially I worked part time in both places for a while. A few years later, I left my post as Smoking Cessation Service Lead to work part time as a research assistant in chronic pain whilst obtaining my PhD in Pain psychology at the University of Leicester. This role also involved me being the module leader for the Psychological Aspects of Pain module in their MSc Pain Management.
After obtaining my PhD I was offered a full-time role at Milton Keynes Hospital and gradually grew the psychology service providing both one-to-one psychologically therapy, group therapy and pain management programme. As the service became more successful, evidenced by outcome measures we were able to recruit other psychologists and have trainees on placement. After my PhD I continued to study different therapeutic approaches to give more treatment options to our patients. I contributed to the local service development of community pain clinics and those in different parts of the country. Over time, I worked my way up to Consultant Health Psychologist. I have served on committees for The British Psychological Society and The British Pain Society and regularly present posters and run workshops at The British Pain Society ASM. Although well out of my comfort zone, this networking lead to some interesting discussions, opportunities, and friendships. In addition to pain

psychology services, I also used to work in oncology with people living with and beyond cancer. I was involved in intensive care after-care programmes and often called upon for general advice regarding psychological aspects of care of patients throughout the hospital.

In March 2017, I left the NHS, it was one of the hardest decisions I have ever made and took me two years to plan. One of the reasons I left was due to lack of support for the pain clinic by the management who never bothered to attend meetings so decisions to move the service forward were never made. However, the main reason to leave was because I couldn't treat my patients in the best way that they deserved to be treated and for me that wasn't acceptable.

Prior to leaving the NHS, I started increasing my work in private practice and reduced my NHS hours. I attended GP training events sometimes as a speaker, to get myself known. A year into full-time private practice, I'm loving it, although sometimes it is a challenge to fulfil the admin roles! I see a wide range of patients including those with chronic pain, and cancer, but also anxiety, insomnia, mild depression, and fears/phobias, so I can use the wide range of therapeutic techniques I have gained. Also, I undertake medico-legal work which is a fascinating area. I have written a few books, write regular blogs, contribute to various charity newsletters and am developing online products. In addition to presenting to medical colleagues, I'm out and about speaking at various support groups and WI groups which is fantastic to get psychology out into the public arena.

I'm looking forward to what the future will bring!


**Dr Sue Peacock, Consultant Health Psychologist**

www.apaininthemind.co.uk

www.well-ahead.com

# The 1st C
## Is for
# Conviction

**Beliefs: Opinions: Views**

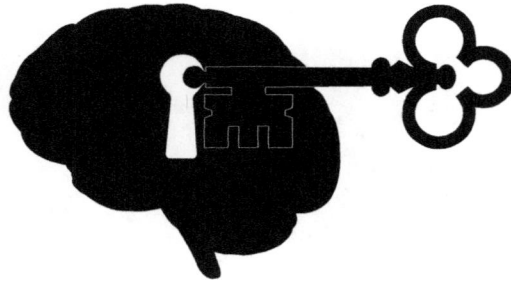

# Belief Systems

> **"We all have our time machines.**
> **Some take us back. They're called memories.**
> **Some take us forward. They're called dreams."**
>
> **Jeremy Irons**

## Aims

The aim of this chapter is for you to have more of an understanding of what belief systems are, how they are formed and how they impact you on every aspect of your life.

## Objectives

The objective is for you to read the chapter and complete the given exercises to help you recognise what old, outdated, limiting and unhelping beliefs you are currently holding onto and maintaining.
How? By getting you to examine your belief systems in greater detail. By looking at those significant people and situations of the past, that have been responsible for your current way of thinking, feeling, and behaving.

**Goal Setting**

1. What goals are you hoping to achieve from completing this chapter?

2. What might help you in achieving this?

3. Is what you want to achieve realistic, and within your scope or abilities/capabilities?

4. What has stopped you before in the past?

5. Why will this time be different for you?

6. How different would your life be, if you did achieve what you set out to achieve?

7. How would you know if you were successful in achieving it?

---

**Time to think, reflect and to record your findings here:**

The term 'belief system' comes from the world of psychology, and describes a person's individual collection of skills, knowledge, understandings, and perceptions of what they have learned throughout their lives. This is achieved through repetition, which in turn creates a habitual way of thinking, feeling, and behaving.

Our belief systems give us our own sense of reality and helps us function on a day-to-day basis. We literally have a belief system for everything we currently think, feel, act, or react to.

If you think about it, we are constantly bombarded with never-ending streams of information, to assimilate, act upon, or reject. So, by having our own internal filtering system, we can process this information much more easily and effectively. How? By easily and effortlessly seeing if we have experienced the situation before, without any conscious awareness. And if we have experienced what we are currently experiencing, we then measure what emotional response it produced, and what the result was from having that experience. If we have not experienced what we are currently experiencing before, we will then create a brand-new belief system based on this new experience. And once again, through repetition, you will transform this belief system into a newly-formed habit, which then drives our thoughts, feelings, actions, and behaviours.

So, in a nutshell; we could say our belief systems are simply habitual responses, based on repeating the emotional response from past experiences in the current situation.

So, where do these belief systems come from? Let us start at the very beginning of our lives. Imagine when we were born, we all had "installed" pre-birth, filed away in the primitive part of our mind or brain, some very basic primary beliefs, that we didn't have to consciously think about, but upon which we just acted automatically. These primary belief systems ensured we survived the first few months of life and beyond, (think suckling at the breast or bottle, crying when we needed or wanted attention or comfort etc.). Then, as we grew and developed, we started to become much more consciously aware and curious of the world around us. And wanted to learn and experience more and to understand what was going on around us, so we could understand what was going on from our own perspective, our own point on view or viewpoint.

A study discovered girls aged four are the most curious. Asking an incredible 390 questions per day - averaging a question every 1 minute 56 seconds of their waking day.

So, with that in mind, you can understand why we need a robust system to be in place, to enable us start to process, encode and store all this information for future reference. And most importantly, for us to make sense of it through our own eyes, so we can act upon it as we saw fit.

So, where does all this information come from? Every day we are constantly bombarded with information from the world around us. It has been suggested that we take in the equivalent of 174 newspapers worth of information in every day. And all this information comes to us via one of our five senses: sight, sound, smell, taste, and touch, which then evokes an emotional response to the situation. And it is these physical, mental, and emotional constructions from those initial first experiences that then become ingrained into our reality from repetition and habit, which we call memories, that form the basis of our belief systems.

Interestingly, most of our significant belief systems are formed in very early childhood; from the age of 0-5 years old, and then they continue forming up to around the age of 12 years old. This time is called the formative years and is universally considered the most important part of a child's psychological, physiological, and emotional development. It literally paves the way to how they think, feel, act, react, and behave as an adult. Most people have very little recollection of this period in their lives, unless it was a significant experience or memory, such as starting school, getting an injection or physical, mental, or emotional abuse or trauma etc.

So where do these beliefs come from? It can be very helpful, informative, educational, and quite enlightening to know why you believe what you do and where these beliefs have come from.

You might be surprised to realise that some of your belief systems have been formed on shaky ground. They are very likely based on the 5 reasons below:

- **Global Evidential Beliefs** – These beliefs are what I class as global beliefs and are accepted worldwide, as an evidence-based belief system. These belief systems very rarely cause any problems as there is nothing to dispute or challenge e.g. there are 7 days in a week, 12 months in a year, 26 letters in the English alphabet, 9 planets in the solar system etc.

- **Passed Down Traditional Beliefs** – These beliefs are bathed in tradition and superstition, and are often passed down through families, culture, social class, or religion.

- **People of Authority Beliefs** – These beliefs come from people in authority and are often accepted without argument, or are not challenged, such as Doctors, Parents, School Teachers, Religious Leaders, Managers or Bosses.

- **By Association Beliefs** – These beliefs are formed purely by association and are fuelled by who you are friends with, who and where you hang about. Where you share pastimes activities, hobbies, interests, or pursuits and with whom.

- **From Self Beliefs** – These beliefs are based on your own intuition, gut reaction, hunches, and inklings. It is those beliefs you can see in your mind's eye, and imagine the outcome based on your own personal experiences and the imagined outcome. For example, when you imagine yourself changing job, and can envisage yourself doing something completely different, because it feels like it's time for a change.

---

**"Man often becomes what he believes himself to be. If I keep on saying to myself that I cannot do a certain thing, it is possible that I may end by really becoming incapable of doing it. On the contrary, if I shall have the belief that I can do it, I shall surely acquire the capacity to do it, even if I may not have it at the beginning."**
**Mahatma Gandhi**

---

## Exercise One

## Those significant people in your early life

So, let's take a closer look at those significant people who have contributed to your own personal belief systems in your early life.

| | | | |
|---|---|---|---|
| MOTHER<br><br>STEP MOTHER | FATHER<br><br>STEP FATHER | OTHER PRIMARY CAREGIVERs | GRAND PARENTS<br><br>STEP GRAND PARENTS |
| SIBLINGS<br><br>STEP SIBLINGS | AUNTIES | UNCLES | COUSINS |
| FAMILY FRIENDS | NEIGHBOURS | DOCTORS | DENTISTS |
| NURSES | CHILDHOOD FRIENDS | BULLIES | HOBBIES/ PURSUITS LEADERS |
| TEACHERS | PARENTS OF YOUR FRIENDS | SHOP-KEEPERS | HEADMASTER/ HEADMISTRESS |
| PRIEST/ NUN VICAR REVEREND | IMAN | RABBI | OTHER RELIGIOUS INFLUENCES |

## Who were significant figures in your life as a child?

## What beliefs do you hold about them now?

So, you have learned when and how a belief system was formed, and you have looked at those significant people who played a big part in your life as a child. What you find is that it is very common for a significant person from childhood to be part of your current problem. Hence why we look and explore past and present significant others.

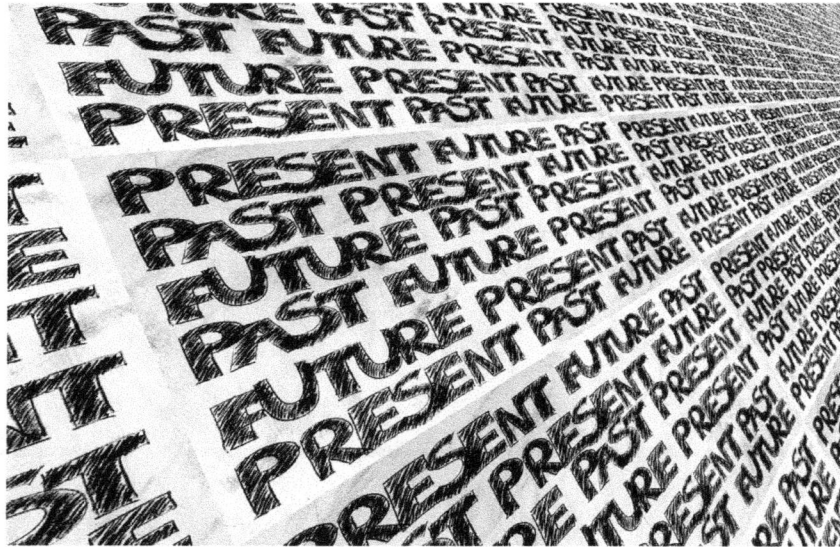

## Something for you to read

**Dental Phobia Case study**

Ben is a 5-year-old little boy, and it is time to have his routine 6-month dental appointment. Ben has been going to the dentist all his life; since he was 18-months old. So, he is very used to going to the dentist on a regular basis. His usual dentist Mr. Smith has retired, and Mr. Jones, is going to be Ben's new dentist instead. Mr. Jones is in a rush that day, because he is very busy with lots of patients to see. He is also very pushed for time, due to an emergency patient before Ben.

Mr. Jones is seeing all his patients in his own room. He doesn't have pictures of the brightly coloured fish on the ceiling like Mr. Smith did. Ben really liked talking about the fish with Mr. Smith, and Mr. Smith found from experience that talking about the fish made Ben laugh. And Ben always felt relaxed looking at them when Mr. Smith was carrying out his examination.

So, this day, Mr. Jones calls Ben into his room, and Ben's mum wants to leave him by himself. But Ben is feeling quite nervous and very apprehensive because it is a new room and new person. So, he asks his mum to stay with him. Mum was quite sharp with Ben, and told him not to be silly, and that he is a big boy now and to go in by himself. Mum had finished work late last night and was looking forward to sitting in the waiting room and read her latest magazine in peace and quiet for 10 minutes. However, after Ben insisted, mum stayed with him, but Ben could feel she was not happy about it. Mum is preoccupied, thinking about what to cook for dinner tonight, and not paying any attention to what Mr. Jones is doing or saying. It took Ben ages to settle down, and because of this, Mr. Jones is in even more of a rush now. Ben is noticing this and is starting to feel even more nervous and apprehensive.

Because of this Ben feels very tense, and when Mr. Jones asks Ben to open his mouth a bit wider, Ben accidently closes his mouth by mistake, and Mr. Smith catches Ben on the lip with one of the dental instruments. Ben cried out in pain and started to hold back his tears. Mr Jones told Ben off for causing a scene and told him not to be a cry baby and carried out the inspection quite briskly. As mum was so preoccupied, she didn't hear what the dentist said, so she didn't defend Ben, or pass any comment about the situation. After Mr Jones had finished his inspection, he curtly told Ben he would see him again in 6-months, and that he hoped he would be better behaved next time and not be as silly as he was today. Same again, mum didn't notice what was being said, as she was concentrating on getting home and preparing the evening meal before getting ready to go to work. Ben left his appointment feeling very subdued and apprehensive about his next appointment with Mr. Smith in 6-months' time. But Ben felt he couldn't tell his mum because he felt she wasn't bothered today. And he didn't want her to think he was being even more silly and stupid than he had been today.

Because Ben didn't have the emotional understanding and rationale at that age, he started to internalise those thoughts, feelings, and emotions, and started to believe that he was silly/stupid, because it was his fault for being scared and being a cry baby. And mum just confirmed it by being sharp with him about staying in the room, and not saying anything when Mr. Jones spoke to him that way.

So next time Ben went to the dentist, all those previous thoughts, feelings, emotions and reactions that made Ben feel very nervous and apprehensive at that time came flooding back. So, Ben then behaved as a nervous and anxious patient. Which just confirmed his beliefs that Dentists equate to fear and pain. And something to be scared of. This in turn will become his reality every time Ben goes to the Dentist in the future. Why? Because it will end up becoming a self-fulfilling prophecy based on his perception of reality and the cycle of his thoughts, feelings, emotions and reactions and the outcome he expects to happen!

So, from this experience, Ben could develop and adopt the following negative, unhelpful, and limiting belief systems:

- I am not brave
- I am a cry baby
- I am stupid
- I am such a silly person
- I am not good enough
- It is all my fault
- Mum doesn't care about me
- Going to the dentist is: -
    - Stressful
    - Anxiety-provoking
    - Nerve-racking
    - Painful
    - Excruciating
    - Agonising
    - Awful
    - Dreadful
    - Terrible
    - Horrible
    - Nasty
    - Terrifying
    - Scary

You can see now why so many adults don't like going to the dentist!

**Is there anything you recognised about yourself from the case study? Or from one of your own personal life experiences? Record your findings below:**

### Exercise Two

**Those significant contributory situations in your early life**

So, we have looked at those significant people who played a big part in your life as a child and in early childhood.

Now we are going to have a look at those situations that have contributed to your past and present belief systems and is contributing to your problem.

| Upbringing | School | Family |
|---|---|---|
| Work | Parenthood | Religious Influences |
| Divorce | Separation | Education |
| Unemployment | Prison | Redundancy |
| Hobbies | Moving House | Changing Schools |
| Friendships | Peer Pressure | Being Bullied |
| Marriage | Relationships | Illness |
| Money | Wealth | Debt |
| Sex | Intimacy | Performance |
| Disability | Death | Loss |
| Abuse - Mental | Abuse - Emotional | Abuse – Physical |
| Trauma | Physical and Emotional Pain | Violence |

## What were significant situations in your life as a child?

## What beliefs do you hold about them now?

## The Dancing Monkeys

A Prince had some monkeys trained to dance. Being naturally great mimics of men's actions, they showed themselves most apt pupils, and when arrayed in their rich clothes and masks, they danced as well as any of the courtiers. The spectacle was often repeated with great applause, until on one occasion a courtier, bent on mischief, took from his pocket a handful of nuts and threw them upon the stage. The monkeys at the sight of the nuts forgot their dancing and became (as indeed they were) monkeys instead of actors. Pulling off their masks and tearing off their robes, they fought with one another for the nuts. The dancing spectacle thus came to an end amidst the laughter and ridicule of the audience.

The morale of the story is not everything you see is what it appears to be.

*From Aesop's Fables*

### Exercise Three

**Looking at your beliefs around work, study, education, and career**

So, we have looked at those significant people who played a big part in your life as a child and in early childhood. And we have had a look at those situations that have contributed to your past and present belief systems.

In this exercise we are going to examine your beliefs around what you think about going to college, university, getting an apprenticeship, finding a job, or pursuing a career that you currently hold.

| | | |
|---|---|---|
| I am not bright enough to … | Only rich, or really brainy people go to university | I am not clever enough to … |
| No-one in me family has ever … | The career I want is out of my reach because … | It is expected that I … |
| The men/women in my family have always … | I am going to find it far too difficult to … | My friends/family don't think I would be good at … |
| I am far too stupid to … | People like me don't get the good/best paid jobs | I have been told not to go above my station |
| Doing an apprenticeship is cheap labour | My family would be disappointed if I … | You must go to university, to get yourself a good job |
| You must be brainy, to be successful in work | No-one would employ me, as I have no experience | Nobody gets a good job after going to college or university |
| I was told I won't amount to anything | I am no good at studying | I am far too old to change now |

**What unhelpful or limiting beliefs did you recognise in yourself? Record your thoughts here:**

## Can you swim?

I [John Ellerthorpe] once heard of a story of a professor who was being ferried across a river by a boatman, who was no scholar.

So, the professor said, "Can you write, my man?"
"No, sir," said the boatman.
"Then you have lost one third of your life," said the professor.

"Can you read?" again asked he of the boatman.
"No," replied the latter, "I can't read."
"Then you have lost the half of your life," said the professor.

Now came the boatman's turn. "Can you swim?" said the boatman to the professor.
"No," was his reply.

"Then," said the boatman, "you have lost the whole of your life, for the boat is sinking and you'll be drowned."

**Exercise Four**

# Perspective

## Looking at the world from another point of view

Perspective: From the from Latin *Perspectus* – meaning clearly perceived.

The idea of this exercise is to help you look at things from another perspective. That is another angle, another way of seeing things. Another point of view.

To change our beliefs, we must start to change the way we currently think, feel, act, or behave. And to start looking at the situation from another perspective.

And the wonderful thing about this exercise is there is no right or wrong, but only your own perspective on what you think, feel, or believe you are seeing or experiencing!

---

**"Everything we hear is an opinion, not a fact.
Everything we see is a perspective, not the truth."**

**Marcus Aurelius**

---

# Let us have a look at what you think you see?

Is the photographer suspended in the air, or does he have both feet on the ground or is he lying on the ground?

Is the person tall, short, or average height?

Do you see feathers, ice, a reflection, or something else completely?

Is the photographer really that small, or is the standing block the lady standing on very high? Or is the lady extremely tall?

What do you see?  Dogs, a deer, the moon, or a child?

Are the people going up or down the steps?

**Time to think, reflect and to record your findings here:**

## Something for you to read

Below is an old Chinese fable about having perspective on the good things and bad things that happen to us in life.

There once was a farmer. One day the farmer's only horse broke out of the corral and ran away. The farmer's neighbors, all hearing of the horse running away, came to the farmer's house to view the corral. As they stood there, the neighbors all said, "Oh what bad luck!" The farmer replied, "Perhaps."

About a week later, the horse returned, bringing with it a whole herd of wild horses, which the farmer and his son quickly corralled. The neighbors, hearing of the corralling of the horses, came to see for themselves. As they stood there looking at the corral filled with horses, the neighbors said, "Oh what good luck!" The farmer replied, "Perhaps."

A couple of weeks later, the farmer's son's leg was badly broken when he was thrown from a horse he was trying to break. A few days later the broken leg became infected and the son became delirious with fever. The neighbors, all hearing of the incident, came to see the son. As they stood there, the neighbors said, "Oh what bad luck!" The farmer replied, "Perhaps."

At that same time in China, a war broke out between two rival warlords. In need of more soldiers, a captain came to the village to conscript young men to fight in the war. When the captain came to take the farmer's son, he found the young man with a broken leg--delirious with fever. Knowing there was no way the son could fight, the captain left him there. A few days later, the son's fever broke. The neighbors, hearing of the son's not being taken to fight in the war and of his return to good health, all came to see him. As they stood there, each one said, "Oh what good luck!" The farmer replied, "Perhaps."

**Time to think, reflect and to record your findings here:**

**Exercise Four**

# The ABCDE Cycle to Change

### A = Activating Event
This is the initial trigger, stimuli, person, event, or situation that starts the initial process of stress, anxiety, discomfort, or pain

### B = Beliefs
These are the beliefs you hold around (A) – the activating event

### C = Consequences
These are the consequences that result from (A) the activating event and (B) your beliefs around it e.g. fear, anger, disappointment, jealousy or depression

### D = Disputing
This is where you start to dispute your beliefs (B) relating to the activating event (A)

### E = Effect
This is where you take a step back and look at the situation from another perspective. When you do this, you get a different effect, that gives you a different result.

---

**"Insanity: Doing the same thing over and over again.
And expecting a different result."**

**Albert Einstein**

---

# What do you recognise you need or want to change - through the ABCDE Model?

A =

B =

C =

D =

E =

## All the Difference in The World

Every Sunday morning, I take a light jog around a park near my home. There's a lake located in one corner of the park. Each time I jog by this lake, I see the same elderly woman sitting at the water's edge with a small metal cage sitting beside her.

This past Sunday my curiosity got the best of me, so I stopped jogging and walked over to her. As I got closer, I realized that the metal cage was in fact a small trap. There were three turtles, unharmed, slowly walking around the base of the trap. She had a fourth turtle in her lap that she was carefully scrubbing with a spongy brush.

"Hello," I said. "I see you here every Sunday morning. If you don't mind my nosiness, I'd love to know what you're doing with these turtles."

She smiled. "I'm cleaning off their shells," she replied. "Anything on a turtle's shell, like algae or scum, reduces the turtle's ability to absorb heat and impedes its ability to swim. It can also corrode and weaken the shell over time."

"Wow! That's really nice of you!" I exclaimed.

She went on: "I spend a couple of hours each Sunday morning, relaxing by this lake and helping these little guys out. It's my own strange way of making a difference."

"But don't most freshwater turtles live their whole lives with algae and scum hanging from their shells?" I asked.

"Yep, sadly, they do," she replied.

I scratched my head. "Well then, don't you think your time could be better spent? I mean, I think your efforts are kind and all, but there are fresh water turtles living in lakes all around the world. And 99% of these turtles don't have kind people like you to help them clean off their shells. So, no offense... but how exactly are your localised efforts here truly making a difference?"

The woman giggled aloud. She then looked down at the turtle in her lap, scrubbed off the last piece of algae from its shell, and said, "Sweetie, if this little guy could talk, he'd tell you I just made all the difference in the world."

**The moral:** You can change the world – maybe not all at once, but one person, one animal, and one good deed at a time. Wake up every morning and pretend like what you do makes a difference. It does.

**Your plan of action:**

1.  What have you learned from completing this chapter?

2.  What are you going to do next to improve/better yourself?

3.  Is what you want to achieve realistic, and within your scope or abilities/capabilities?

4.  How would you know if you were successful in achieving it?

"A belief system usually evolves over time. It's something that we grow into, as our needs and goals develop and change. Even when we find a system of beliefs that works for us, we hone and fine-tune it, working our way deeper and deeper into its essential truth.

Everything we experience, every thought we have, every desire, need, action, and reaction - everything we perceive with our senses goes into our personal databank and helps to create the belief systems that we hold now. Nothing is lost or forgotten in our lives.

You don't have to remain a victim of your conditioning, however. You can choose for yourself what you believe or don't believe, what you desire and don't desire. You can define your own parameters. Once you do that, you can start consciously creating your destiny according to your own vision."

Skye Alexander

*The modern guide to Witchcraft: Your complete guide to witches, covens, and spells*

# The 2nd C
## Is for
# Cognition

**Thoughts: Knowledge: Understanding**

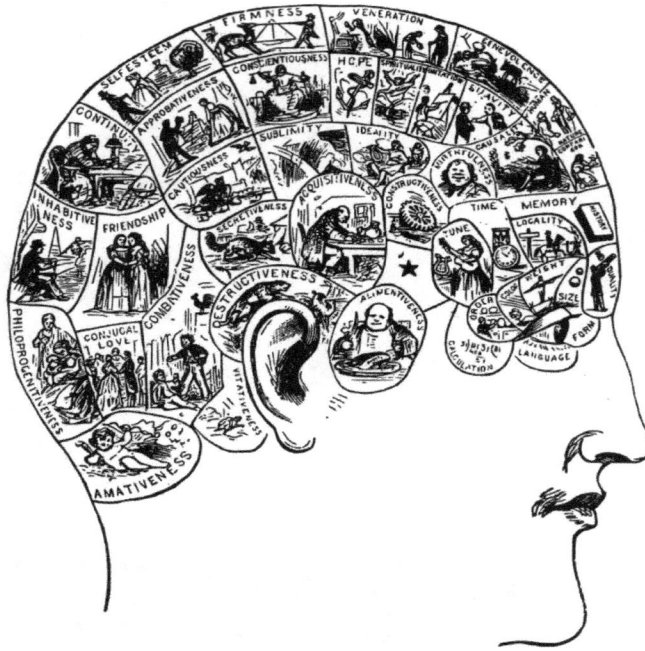

# What are you thinking?

"Whether you think you can, or you think you can't –
you're right."

Henry Ford

## Aims

The aim of this chapter is for you to have more of an understanding of thinking.

## Objectives

The objective is for you to read the chapter and complete the given exercises to help change the way you think, feel, and believe in yourself. How? By managing your thinking more effectively.

**Let us reflect on what you want to achieve from this chapter here:**

1. **Thinking** – noun - the process of considering or reasoning about something

2. **Thinking** – adjective - using thought or rational judgement; intelligence

The word **Thinking** comes from PIE (Proto-Indo-European) Tongue – meaning "to *think*, feel", which also is the root of Thought and Thank.

The word **Cognition** stems from the Latin *Cognit* – meaning "getting to know, acquaintance, knowledge". And later from mid-15c Old English we got the word Cognitive – which means "ability to comprehend, think and awareness.

## So, what is thinking?

Thinking is the mental processes that we apply when we seek to make sense of an experience from the world around us, based on past experiences. These thinking skills enable us to integrate each new and old experience by constructing the concept of "how things are or should be" into our existing belief systems.

It is apparent that better thinking will help us to learn more from our experiences, and to make better use of our lives and the opportunities available to us.

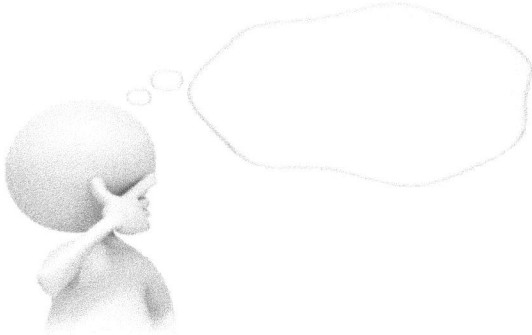

## Unhelpful Thinking Styles and Cognitive Distortions

Over the years, as a form of mental, emotional, or psychological protection, we have learned to protect ourselves from perceived or actual threats, attitudes, or assumptions from ourselves and others. And it is those unhelpful thinking styles, thinking habits and cognitive distortions that our mind convinces us of something, that isn't true, or is, or is not an actual reality, to the current situation.

So, an unhelpful thinking style refers to that biased, unrealistic, and limiting habitual way of thinking about oneself and the current situation.

Once you can start to identify and notice your very own habitual unhelpful thinking styles and cognitive distortions, then you can start to challenge or distance yourself from those unhelpful thoughts, attitudes, and assumptions that have been causing you a problem. And start to see the situation in a different and more helpful way.

---

**"Believing in negative thoughts
is the single greatest obstruction to success."**

**Charles F. Glassman**

---

Listed below are the most common unhelpful thinking styles and cognitive distortions that people tend to exhibit:

## Filtering

Filtering is where we take the negative details and magnify them while filtering out all positive aspects of a situation.

Imagine a situation where a person may pick out a single, unpleasant detail and dwell on it exclusively, so that their vision of reality becomes darkened or distorted.

Filtering statement examples:

- **The negative**
- **What they missed or didn't achieve**
- **What went wrong**

**What are your thoughts? Do you recognise yourself here?**

## Polarised or Black & White Thinking

In polarised thinking, things are either "black-or-white — there is no middle ground, and you place people or situations in "either/or" categories, with no shades of grey.

This unhelpful thinking style is extremely rigid in its making and does not allow for the complexity of most people and situations. And has its roots firmly in trying to control the situation.

Black & White Thinkers tend to think in absolutes, for example, everything is either "every, "always" or "never":

Black & White statement examples:

- **Good or bad**
- **Right or wrong**
- **Sad or happy**

**What are your thoughts? Do you recognise yourself here?**

## Over-generalisation

Over-generalisation happens when we come to a general conclusion based on a single incident or a single piece of evidence.

That is, if something bad happens only once, we expect it to happen over, and over again.

A person who over-generalises tends to see a single, unpleasant event as part of a never-ending pattern of defeat.

Over-generalisation example statements:

- **He / she always**
- **Everyone**
- **You never**

**What are your thoughts? Do you recognise yourself here?**

## Global Labelling

Global labelling is when we generalise one or two qualities into a negative global judgment either about ourselves or about others.

Instead of describing an error in context of a specific situation, a person will attach an unhealthy label to themselves or reflect it onto another person, that is completely overboard and often unwarranted.

**Global Labelling example statements:**

- **I am / am not**
- **I can / cannot**
- **I will / will not**

**What are your thoughts? Do you recognise yourself here?**

## Blaming

Blaming is when we either hold other people responsible for our problems. Or where we blame ourselves for every problem going.

The truth is, nobody can "make" us feel in any way.

It is only ourselves that have control over our own emotions, reactions, and behaviours towards ourselves and others.

Blaming example statements:

- **I must**
- **I have to**
- **I really should**

**What are your thoughts? Do you recognise yourself here?**

## Jumping to conclusions

Jumping to conclusions is all about pre-empting what a person is going to say, do or feel about a situation, without any kind of evidence.

And when a person jumps to conclusions, then they don't bother to find out if they are correct or not, but just go on the assumption they are right.

Jumping to conclusion statement examples:

- **I will never**
- **This is never going to**
- **I know it is going to happen**

**What are your thoughts? Do you recognise yourself here?**

**+**

## Catastrophising

When a person catastrophises, they expect disaster to strike at any time, no matter what. This is also referred to as "magnifying or minimising."

When a person catastrophises, they blow the situation completely out of proportion, and quite often or not use dramatic and catastrophising language, facial and hand expressions, and actions to fuel the thought and belief even further.

Catastrophising thinking example statements:

- **This is really, really awful**
- **I am absolutely devastated**
- **This is so bad, I just don't know what to do**

**What are your thoughts? Do you recognise yourself here?**

## Personalisation

Personalisation is where a person believes that everything others do or say, is a direct personal attack, reaction, or retaliation to them.

They often see themselves as the cause of some external event or situation that they were not responsible for.

Personalisation example statements:

- **If I was a**
- **I must have done something wrong**
- **It is all my fault that**

---

**What are your thoughts? Do you recognise yourself here?**

## Always being right

With this unhelpful thinking style, the person is continually trying to prove that their opinions and actions are correct. To them, being wrong is unthinkable and they will go to any length to demonstrate how right they are.

Being right often is more important than the feelings of others around, even loved ones in this cognitive distortion. People like this can quite often be thought of as being arrogant, cocky or overconfident. Or even a bit of a know all.

Always being right example statements:

- **I told you so**
- **Just listen to me**
- **That is not right**

**What are your thoughts? Do you recognise yourself here?**

## Perfectionism

A perfectionistic thinking style is characterised by a person's striving for unrealistic and quite often unobtainable and unachievable high standards. That is accompanied by critical self-evaluations and concerns regarding others' evaluations and perceptions of what they are trying to achieve or obtain.

Perfectionism or Perfectionistic example statements:

- **I have to**
- **I must**
- **I have got to**

**What are your thoughts? Do you recognise yourself here?**

# Emotional Reasoning

Emotional reasoning assumes that what we think or believe we are feeling must be automatically true, based on the assumption of because I am thinking about it and / or physically feeling it – therefore it must be true.

For example, if I think and feel stupid and boring, then I must be stupid and boring

Emotional reasoning example statements:

- **I feel ugly, so I must be ugly**
- **I believe I am stupid, so therefore I must be stupid**
- **I feel like I am never going achieve anything in life, so I won't**

**What are your thoughts? Do you recognise yourself here?**

## Should, Must or Ought

When we live a life with a list of ironclad rules about how we, and others should, must or ought to behave. Then this is quite often very stressful and anxiety provoking.

And should we or others break these rules, this makes us feel very guilty and a failure. And this in turn make us angry because these rules have been violated.

However, when we direct a should statement toward another, this is often promoting feelings of anger, frustration, and resentment, because quite often we are not getting what we truly want or desire.

Should statement examples:

- **I should**
- **I must**
- **I ought**

**What are your thoughts? Do you recognise yourself here?**

## Fallacy of Control

The fallacy of control is believing we are responsible for the pain and happiness of everyone around us.

And thus, we try desperately hard to control the situation but often, not managing to achieve it.

Fallacy of control example statements:

- **I can't help it, you made me do it, and now you are angry**
- **It is not my fault. I only did what you asked me to do**
- **Why are you not happy? Is it something I did?**

**What are your thoughts? Do you recognise yourself here?**

## Fallacy of Fairness

The fallacy of fairness has us feeling resentful because we think we know what is fair, but other people won't or don't agree with us.

People who go through life applying this against every situation, judging it on its "fairness" will often feel bad because of it, and they will have a sense of always being let down by life.

Fallacy of Fairness example statements:

- **It's not fair**
- **Why does it always happen to me?**
- **Can't you see what is happening?**

**What are your thoughts? Do you recognise yourself here?**

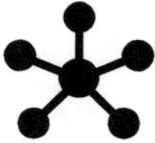

## Fallacy of Change

With the fallacy of change, we expect that other people will change to suit us if we pressure, cajole, or manipulate them enough.

With the fallacy of change we believe we need to change people, because our hopes for happiness depend entirely on them.

Fallacy of Change example statements:

- **Why won't he / she change?**
- **Why can't they do it my way?**
- **If they could only see how unhappy this is making me**

**What are your thoughts? Do you recognise yourself here?**

## Fallacy of a Heavenly Reward

With the fallacy of a heavenly reward, we expect our sacrifices to pay off with a reward or recognition of some kind. As we believe that input is equal to output. By putting everything and everyone before ourselves. We give out so much good karma that good things "must" come back to us.

However, we can feel very bitter and betrayed when our reward doesn't come to fruition and our sacrifice is not recognised or has been played down.

Fallacy of a Heavenly reward example statements:

- **What goes around comes around – it's Karma**
- **All of my good deeds will pay off one day**
- **You reap what you sow**

**What are your thoughts? Do you recognise yourself here?**

# Below is a selection of famous quotes. Do you agree or disagree with them?

- "There is nothing either good or bad but thinking makes it so".
  William Shakespeare

- "Very little is needed to make a happy life; it is all within yourself, in your way of thinking".
  Marcus Aurelius

- "We cannot solve our problems with the same thinking we used when we created them".
  Albert Einstein

- "Positive thinking will let you do everything better than negative thinking will".
  Zig Ziglar

- "Self-worth comes from one thing - thinking that you are worthy".
  Wayne Dyer

- "Thinking is the hardest work there is, which is probably the reason why so few engage in it."
  Henry Ford

- "Positive thinking is the notion that if you think good thoughts, things will work out well. Optimism is the feeling of thinking things will be well and be hopeful".
  Martin Seligman

- "Studies have shown that 90% of error in thinking is due to error in perception. If you can change your perception, you can change your emotion, and this can lead to new ideas".
  Edward de Bono

- "As long as you're going to be thinking anyway, think big".
  Donald Trump

- "The only real mistake is the one from which we learn nothing."
  Henry Ford

**Exercise One**

**We are what we think – We are what we say – We are what we imagine**

As we have found, the rule of the mind is very clear on this. Our minds/brains like familiarity. So, if we constantly think, tell, or imagine ourselves something over, and over again. Then we are going to accept it as being familiar. And guess what – it will happen. And it will just increase that sense of familiarity and becomes a part of self-acceptance. That is, the belief that this is how it is meant to be. If you think about anything you do regularly in life – it is all born out of habit.

**Thoughts + Images + Action + Repetition = Habit**

In this exercise I would like you to monitor very closely over the next week, what regular negative, unhelpful and unbeneficial thoughts, words, images, and actions (behaviours) you have been saying, thinking, and doing (actions) to yourself and to others. Or what others have been saying or gesturing about you as a person, your abilities, and capabilities. To get the ball rolling, I have put a few down, a few of the more common ones as an example.

| Stupid | Disappointment | Pathetic | Not good enough |
|--------|----------------|----------|-----------------|
|        |                |          |                 |
|        |                |          |                 |
|        |                |          |                 |
|        |                |          |                 |
|        |                |          |                 |
|        |                |          |                 |

# Record your thoughts here:

# Thinking

If you think you are beaten, you are
If you think you dare not, you don't,
If you like to win, but you think you can't
It is almost certain you won't.

If you think you'll lose, you're lost
For out of the world we find,
Success begins with a fellow's will
It's all in the state of mind.

If you think you are outclassed, you are
You've got to think high to rise,
You've got to be sure of yourself before
You can ever win a prize.

Life's battles don't always go
To the stronger or faster man,
But soon or late the man who wins
Is the man WHO THINKS HE CAN!

**A poem by Walter D. Wintle**

Remarkably little is known about Walter D. Wintle except that he was a poet who lived in the late 19th and early 20th century. Nothing is known of the details of his life and indeed the name may in fact be a pseudonym.

He is best known for writing the world-famous poem "Thinking". Or as it is incorrectly titled "The Man Who Thinks He Can".

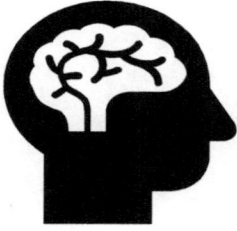

## Soft Skills – The Art of Critical Thinking
## The positive side of thinking

The positive side of Critical Thinking, which we are talking about here, is the psychologically-based practical and emotional application of Soft Skills training and coaching.

What are soft skills? Soft skills are a combination of interpersonal and social skills, that include communication skills, character traits, attitudes, career attributes, social intelligence, and emotional intelligence quotients. Amongst other types of skills, knowledge, and attributes, that help you make the most of your personal attributes.

The soft skills training here will teach you how to look at the root origins of the two words, **Critical** (to judge, learn, observe, and critique/review yourself and the situation) and **Thinking** (what we think and feel about it). And learn how to apply critical thinking physically, mentally, and emotionally to make uniformed judgments and problem solve much more effectively.

So, Critical Thinking as a soft skill can be split into two components:

## 1. Logical/Practical

## 2. Personal/Emotional

**Logical/Practical Critical Thinking Skills are when you ...**
- Are good at making observations
- Can sustain focus
- Tests facts
- Use the necessary tools to assess objectively
- Understand the logical connections between ideas
- Detect inconsistencies and common mistakes through reasoning
- Solve problems systematically
- Understand the relevance and importance of having ideas
- Understand the importance on acting on those ideas
- Think outside-of-the-box
- Constructively task build


**Personal/Emotional Critical Thinking Skills are when you ...**
- Have personal discipline
- Challenge your assumptions
- Reflect on the justification of your own beliefs and values
- Do not believe everything you have been told, or have read
- Identify, constructs, and (re) evaluate an argument
- Strengthen an argument
- Are not afraid to expose fallacies
- Continue developing your strengths
- Work on your weaknesses
- Continue to learn
- Continuously improve your knowledge base
- Build up your resilience
- Are open and receptive to creativity
- Improve the way you express your ideas
- Love being curious

## Exercise Two

**You say tomato – I say tomatoes**

They say opposites attract. But sometimes you need a middle ground to get the solution or an answer to a problem that is not always just so black and white. To achieve this, sometimes you need to change perspective completely, and look at things from a slightly different angle.

In this exercise, I would like you to think of middle ground word, that either compliments, goes with, or balances the two opposing words out either side. There are no right or wrong answers in this exercise. Only different ways at looking at things. To get the ball rolling again, I have put down an example from my own perspective.

| Black | Grey | White |
|---|---|---|
| Good | | Bad |
| Ugly | | Beautiful |
| Logical | | Creative |
| Comb | | Nails |
| Car | | Bicycle |
| Dog | | Tree |
| Fear | | Excitement |
| Mathematics | | Poetry |
| Apple | | Desk |

**Record your thoughts here:**

## The Raven and the Swan

A Raven saw a Swan and desired to secure for himself the same beautiful plumage.

Supposing that the Swan's splendid white colour arose from his washing in the water in which he swam, the Raven left the altars in the neighbourhood where he picked up his living and took up residence in the lakes and pools.

But cleansing his feathers as often as he would, he could not change their colour, while through want of food he perished.

The moral of the story is change of habit cannot alter nature

*From Aesop's Fables*

**Your plan of action:**

1. What have you learned from completing this chapter?

2. What are you going to do next to improve/better yourself?

3. Is what you want to achieve realistic, and within your scope or abilities/capabilities?

4. How would you know if you were successful in achieving it?

"Your time is limited, so don't waste it living someone else's life. Don't be trapped by dogma - which is living with the results of other people's thinking. Don't let the noise of others' opinions drown out your own inner voice. And most important, have the courage to follow your heart and intuition."

**Steve Jobs**

## Inspiration Time

Please find below, an inspiration piece, that was written by my sister Jill Cassidy. This piece reflects her hard work, determination, motivation, and positive thinking, that has gotten her where she is today, working for a leading UK Bank in a Senior Project Management role.

"I left school at 16 with just a few O Levels to my name. All I wanted to do was go out to work to earn some money to pay for driving lessons and a holiday. My first job was processing cheques which I soon realised wasn't challenging enough.

My big break came when I got offered a job at NatWest Bank as a Cashier. By this time, I was 18 years old, and I knew that I wanted to learn and have a career. I was encouraged to go to night school and pass my banking exams and then I found a great mentor who coached me through the ranks. My degree with Honours was funded through work, as were other professional qualifications such as accountancy and trade finance.

It was hard work, working full time, running a house, and studying, but it gave me a great sense of achievement and built resilience.

30 years on and I am still working full time for NatWest and still studying. I have just taken a week's course to learn all about LEAN Project methodology. I now have the title "Senior Manager " and I am confident that having that drive and desire to learn has me where I am career wise.

It's never too late to learn".

**Jill Cassidy – 2018**

# The 3rd C
## Is for
# Communication

**Imparting: Giving: Exchanging**

# Communication

> "To effectively communicate, we must realize that we are all different in the way we perceive the world and use this understanding as a guide to our communication with others".
>
> **Tony Robbins**

## Aims

The aim of this chapter is for you to have more of an understanding of the different types of communication, and how you communicate with yourself and with others determines the life you are going to lead.

## Objectives

The objective is for you to read the chapter and complete the given exercises to help change the way you communicate with yourself and with others. How? By understanding more about verbal and non-verbal language, body language, appearance and self-talk, and the impact it has on you and on other people.

**Let us reflect on what you want to achieve from this chapter here:**

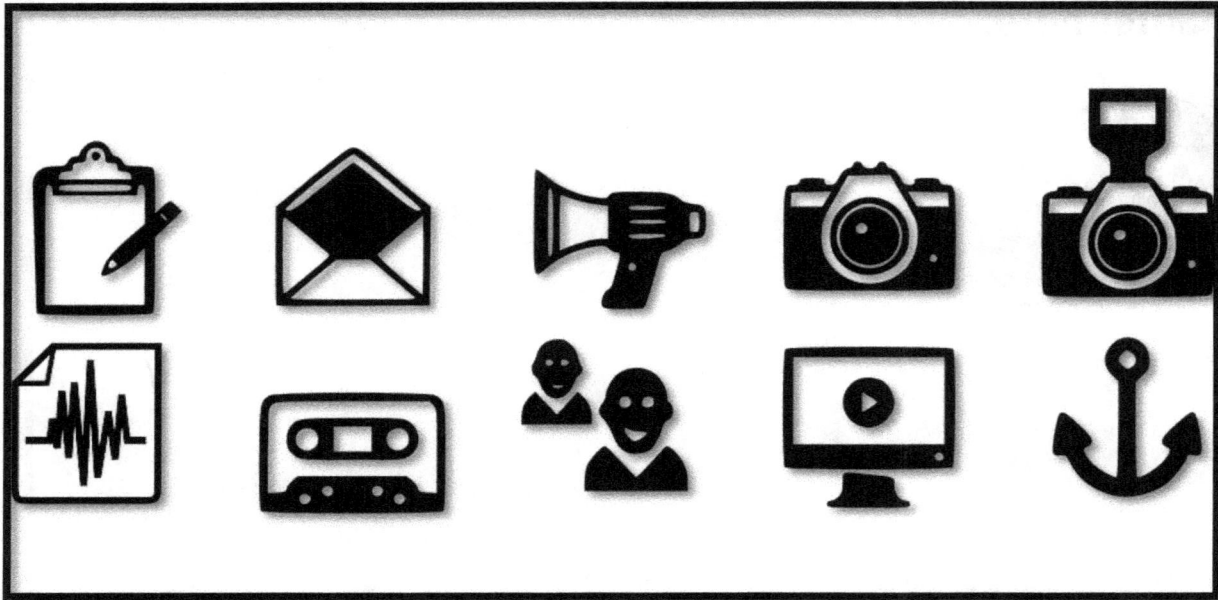

# Communication

The word **Communication** comes from the two Latin words - *Communis* and *Communicare*.

*Communis* as a noun names a person, place, thing, or idea, and in this context means common, communality, or sharing.

*Communicare* as a verb, describes an action, state, or occurrence which in this context, takes *Communicare* to mean to make something common.

In today's hectic world, we rely heavily on the sharing of information, which means greater emphasis is placed on having good, solid communication skills. Good verbal, written and listening communication skills are essential to deliver and receive information easily, quickly, and accurately. Also, we need to read another person's body language and facial cues to ensure we are reading the messages given correctly.

In contrast, poor communication skills can have a negative impact on a person's life; or on the people they are trying to communicate with. This could be the business they work for, the job they do, the career and life that they want or the money they want to earn.

So, good communication is all about how well this information is transmitted, received, and interpreted on both sides.

Like the saying goes, it's not what you say or do, but how it is interpreted that really counts. A poorly-delivered or executed message may result in a misunderstanding, frustration and in some cases cause a real physical, mental, emotional, psychological, or financial disaster.

So, what is meant by communication? By definition; if we look at the root, communication means two or more people, exchanging information to understand each other effectively. So therefore, communication is the process of finding a common denominator in sending and receiving messages, so that both parties can understand what the other person is trying to communicate.

This is achieved through six basic types of communication methods:

1. **Verbal Communication** - In which you listen to a person to understand their meaning

2. **Written Communication** - In which you read their meaning

3. **Visual Communication** – In which images, symbols and graphics show you their meaning

4. **Non-verbal Communication** - In which you observe a person and infer meaning

5. **Appearance Communication** – In which you communicate to others through the power of your appearance

6. **Self–Talk Communication** – In which you communicate to, and with yourself

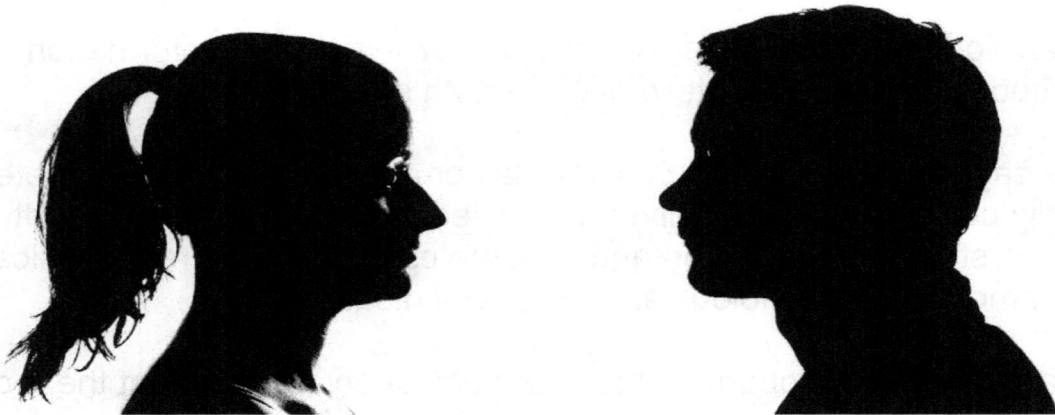

So, what we can surmise is communication involves a sender and a receiver (or receivers) creating, conveying, and exchanging information through various communication channels, that all involved can understand.

Let us have a look at the six styles of communication more closely. And see what those communication styles can bring to make life easier, happier, healthier, and more fulfilling.

## 1. Verbal Communication

Verbal, oral or spoken communication is the act of sharing information between individuals, by using speech, language, or sound. Any interaction that makes use of sound is considered as verbal communication.

Listed below are some examples of verbal communication methods:

- Face-to-Face conversation
- Telephone
- Voice chat
- Video conferencing
- Conference calls
- Voice recordings
- Voicemail
- Skype
- Vlogging
- Lectures
- Conferences
- Presentations
- Public Speaking
- Gossip
- Chit Chat
- Chat Rooms
- Groups
- Acting
- Singing

> **"Wise men speak because they have something to say;
> Fools because they have to say something".**
> **Plato**

## Exercise One

## Are you sure what you are saying, is what you really mean?

**Homophone** – From the Greek, Homos meaning Same, and Phone meaning sound.

A homophone is where two or more words have the same sound and pronunciation. But have different meanings, origins, or spelling.

Listed below are 20 meanings of 2 homophonic words listed.

**Exercise**: Please put what you think is the correct meaning from the **A** or **B** list below.

| | | | |
|---|---|---|---|
| 1 | a person who will legally receive money, property, or a title from another person <br><br> **A or B** | 11 | the expression of sorrow for someone's death <br><br> **A or B** |
| 2 | a device for slowing or stopping a moving vehicle <br><br> **A or B** | 12 | a rounded knotty depression in the centre of a person's belly <br><br> **A or B** |
| 3 | a body of people presided over by a judge, judges, or magistrate <br><br> **A or B** | 13 | a naturally occurring solid material from which a metal or valuable mineral can be extracted <br><br> **A or B** |
| 4 | a person, animal, or plant that stops living <br><br> **A or B** | 14 | a light theatrical entertainment consisting of a series of short sketches, songs, and dances <br><br> **A or B** |
| 5 | a tall, rounded vase with a stem and base <br><br> **A or B** | 15 | plant (seed) by scattering it on, or in the earth <br><br> **A or B** |
| 6 | any other domesticated bird kept for its eggs or flesh <br><br> **A or B** | 16 | a series of rows or levels of a structure placed one above the other <br><br> **A or B** |

| | | | | |
|---|---|---|---|---|
| 7 | a large group of animals<br><br>**A or B** | 17 | unwarranted or inappropriate because excessive or disproportionate | |
| 8 | a person avoiding work; lazy<br><br>**A or B** | 18 | differ in size, amount, degree, or nature from something else of the same general class<br>**A or B** | |
| 9 | in the Middle Ages, a man who served his sovereign or lord as a mounted soldier in armour<br><br>**A or B** | 19 | use or expend carelessly, extravagantly, or to no purpose<br><br>**A or B** | |
| 10 | a plucked stringed instrument<br><br><br>**A or B** | 20 | a part of a garment that fits over the shoulders and to which the main part of the garment is attached<br>**A or B** | |

## Is the meaning A or B?

1.      (A) Air or (B) Heir
2.      (A) Brake or (B) Break
3.      (A) Caught or (B) Court
4.      (A) Dies or (B) Dyes
5.      (A) Earn or (B) Urn
6.      (A) Foul or (B) Fowl
7.      (A) Heard or (B) Herd
8.      (A) Idle or (B) Idol
9.      (A) Knight or (B) Night
10.     (A) Loot or (B) Lute
11.     (A) Morning or (B) Mourning
12.     (A) Navel or (B) Naval
13.     (A) Oar or (B) Ore
14.     (A) Review or (B) Revue
15.     (A) Sew, So or (B) Sow
16.     (A) Tear or (B) Tier
17.     (A) Undo or (B) Undue
18.     (A) Vary or (B) Very
19.     (A) Waist or (B) Waste
20.     (A) Yoke or (B) Yolk

**Answers:**     1 (B), 2 (A), 3 (B), 4 (A), 5 (B), 6 (B), 7 (B), 8 (A), 9 (A), 10 (B)

**11 (B), 12 (A), 13 (B), 14 (B), 15 (B), 16 (B), 17 (B), 18 (A), 19 (B), 20 (A)**

**Time to think, reflect and to record your findings here:**

## 2. Written Communication

Written communication is the act of sharing information through the written word. When messages or information are exchanged or communicated in the written form, either through physical writing, typing, or texting, it is called the written word, so therefore a word-based communication system.

Listed below are some examples of written communication methods:

- Letters
- Documents
- Memos
- Blogs
- Diaries
- Journals
- Books
- Poetry
- Lists
- Notes
- E-mails
- Text
- SMS
- Messenger

"Words are singularly the most powerful force available to humanity. We can choose to use this force constructively with words of encouragement, or destructively using words of despair. Words have energy and power with the ability to help, to heal, to hinder, to hurt, to harm, to humiliate and to humble".
**Yehuda Berg**

### Exercise Two

## More than words

Listed below is a written passage. Chances are you will also understand it. It purports that the order of the letters inside a given word doesn't matter, if the first and last letters of each word, are in the right place.

Why? Because the human mind reads words, and not letter-by-letter.

*"Aoccdrnig to a rscheearch at Cmabrigde Uinervtisy, it deosn't mttaer in waht oredr the ltteers in a wrod are, the olny iprmoatnt tihng is taht the frist and lsat ltteers be at the rghit pclae. The rset can be a toatl mses and you can sitll raed it wouthit porbelm. Tihs is bcuseae the huamn mnid deos not raed ervey lteter by istlef, but the wrod as a wlohe."*

Or can you read this passage?

S1M1L4RLY, Y0UR M1ND 15 R34D1NG 7H15 4U70M471C4LLY W17H0U7 3V3N 7H1NK1NG 4B0U7 17.

Or what do all these words have in common?

| alula | wow | racecar | tenet |
|---|---|---|---|
| sagas | level | madam | kayak |
| reviver | refer | redivider | civic |

**Answer**: All the words are a palindrome. That is all the words read the same forwards and backwards.

**Time to think, reflect and to record your findings here:**

## 3. Visual Communication

Visual communication is the form of communication, described as the conveyance of ideas and information, in forms that can be physically seen to be understood. Visual communication is believed to be the type that people rely on most.

Listed below are some examples of visual communication methods:

- Signs
- Symbols
- Images
- Logos
- Drawings
- Illustrations
- Graphic designs
- Films
- Photographs
- Typography
- Maps
- Paintings
- Sketches
- Advertising
- Cartoons/animation
- Colour

---

**"There is more to seeing than simply sensing imagery. Seeing is also dependent upon memory and one's ability to interpret said imagery."**

**Aldous Huxley,1894 –1963**

---

## Exercise Three

## The power of what you see

The following nine pictures are either complete or partial logos of famous well-known companies and brands. Identify the brand or company and put the correct corresponding number in the boxes below.

| | | |
|---|---|---|
|  **Number 1** |  **Number 2** |  **Number 3** |
|  **Number 4** |  **Number 5** |  **Number 6** |
|  **Number 7** |  **Number 8** |  **Number 9** |

| No | Michelin | No | Porsche | No | Nike |
|---|---|---|---|---|---|
| No | Nestle | No | Apple | No | Playboy |
| No | CNN | No | WWF | No | Walt Disney Pictures |

**Answers**: 1 (Playboy), 2 (Nike), 3 (Walt Disney Pictures), 4 (Nestle), 5 (Porsche), 6 (WWF), 7 (CNN), 8 (Apple), 9 (Michelin)

**Time to think, reflect and to record your findings here:**

## The Fox and the Woodcutter

A Fox, running before the hounds, came across a Woodcutter felling an oak and begged him to show him a safe hiding-place.

The Woodcutter advised him to take shelter in his own hut, so the Fox crept in and hid himself in a corner.

The huntsman soon came up with his hounds and inquired of the Woodcutter if he had seen the Fox. He declared that he had not seen him, and yet pointed, all the time he was speaking, to the hut where the Fox lay hidden. The huntsman took no notice of the signs, but believing his word, hastened forward in the chase.

As soon as they were well away, the Fox departed without taking any notice of the Woodcutter: whereon he called to him and reproached him, saying, "You ungrateful fellow, you owe your life to me, and yet you leave me without a word of thanks." The Fox replied, "Indeed, I should have thanked you fervently if your deeds had been as good as your words, and if your hands had not been traitors to your speech."

The moral of the story is there is as much malice in a wink as in a word.

*From Aesop's Fables*

## 4. Non-verbal Communication

Non-verbal communication between people is communication through sending and receiving wordless clues. It includes the use of visual cues such as body language, distance, alongside understand physical actions, reactions, and behavioural messages.

Listed below are some examples of non-verbal communication methods:

- Body language
- Tone, pitch, timbre, and volume of voice
- Posture
- Facial gestures
- Shaking hands
- Patting the back
- Hugging
- Kissing
- Pushing
- Pulling
- Touching
- Eye Contact
- Hand Gestures
- Nodding or shaking the head
- Bowing the head
- Thumbs up
- Smiling
- Frowning
- Personal space

"Listen with your eyes as well as your ears."

Graham Speechley

### Exercise Four

## A picture paints a thousand words

What are these four following scenes saying to you?

**1)**

**2)**

**3)**

**4)**

**Time to think, reflect and to record your findings here:**

# 5. Appearance Communication

*Appearance* communication, like body language is not only physical and visual, but is also a very powerful and receptive communication base too. Judgment can be formed very quickly, with little-to-no verbalisation, but with only those visual and physical cues on display.

Listed below are some examples of appearance communication methods:

- Dress/Clothes
- Fashion sense
- Style
- Shoes
- Hair
- Make-up
- Perfume/Scent/Aftershave
- Handbags/Cases/Bags
- Accessories
- Jewellery
- Colour
- Style
- Posture
- Stature
- Grooming
- Weight
- Age
- Gender
- Race, Creed or Colour

> **"Things are not always as they seem;
> the first appearance deceives many".**
>
> **Phaedrus**

### Exercise Five

## What messages are the 8 images below conveying to you?

1)

2)

3)

4)

5)

6)

7)

8)

**Time to think, reflect and to record your findings here on the 8 images above:**

1.

2.

3.

4.

5.

6.

7.

8.

## 6. Self-Talk Communication

Self-Talk communication is the act or practice of talking to oneself. Either out aloud, silently or mentally, through the thoughts that you think, the words that you say to yourself. And the pictures and images you paint in your mind

Listed below are some examples of self-talk communication methods:

- Should
- Have to
- Must
- Ought to
- Can't
- Try/Trying
- Just
- Only
- But
- Choose
- Want
- Could
- Intend
- Aim
- Can
- Will
- And
- Next time

"When you give yourself permission to communicate what matters to you in every situation you will have peace despite rejection or disapproval. Putting a voice to your soul helps you to let go of the negative energy of fear and regret."

**Shannon L. Alder**

**Exercise Six**

## Mirror, Mirror on the wall

What old, outdated, negative, unhelpful, and limiting messages are you mirroring back to yourself on a daily basis?

Write your messages in the mirror image below.

# Time to think, reflect and to record your findings here:

## Tongue Twisters

A tongue twister is a specific sequence of words, whose rapid, repeated pronunciation of often similar sounding words, are often quite difficult and challenging to say. Even for a native speaker.

Tongue Twisters are an excellent tool that can be used to improve pronunciation in English. And to give you confidence in all matters of communication.

Professional speakers such as actors, politicians, and television/radio hosts and presenters use them all the time to improve on their articulation, dictation, and pronunciation. And as warm-up exercises prior to speaking.

Remember - The key to tongue twisters is not just how fast you say them, but how clearly too. This is achieved through practice, practice and more practice!

Listed below are a collection of hard, classic, and amusing tongue twisters for you to start practising on.

Peter Piper picked a peck of pickled peppers
A peck of pickled peppers Peter Piper picked
If Peter Piper picked a peck of pickled peppers
Where's the peck of pickled peppers Peter Piper picked

These thousand tricky tongue twisters trip thrillingly off the tongue

Betty Botter bought some butter
But she said the butter's bitter
If I put it in my batter, it will make my batter bitter
But a bit of better butter will make my batter better
So 'twas better Betty Botter bought a bit of better butter

Round and round the rugged rock the ragged rascal ran

Silly Sally swiftly shooed seven silly sheep
The seven silly sheep Silly Sally shooed
Shilly-shallied south
These sheep shouldn't sleep in a shack
Sheep should sleep in a shed

The sixth sick sheik's sixth sheep's sick

[According to The Guinness Book of World Records this is the toughest tongue twister - so far.]

All I want is a proper cup of coffee,
Made in a proper copper coffee pot,
I may be off my dot,
But I want a cup of coffee,
From a proper coffee pot,
Tin coffee pots and iron coffee pots,
They're no use to me,
If I can't have a proper cup of coffee,
In a proper copper coffee pot,
I'll have a cup of tea

Amidst the mists and coldest frosts,
With stoutest wrists and loudest boasts,
He thrusts his fists against the posts,
And still insists he sees the ghosts

Ingenious iguanas improvising an intricate impromptu on impossibly-impractical instruments

Three thin thinkers thinking thick thoughtful thoughts

Nine nimble noblemen nibbling nuts

What a to do to die today,
At a minute or two to two,
A thing distinctly hard to say,
And harder still to do,
For they'll beat a tattoo at twenty to two,
A rat-tat-tat-Tat-tat-tat-Tat-tat-tat-too,
And the dragon will come when he hears the drum,
At a minute or two to two today,
At a minute or two to two

Of all the felt I ever felt,
I never felt a piece of felt,
which felt as fine as that felt felt,
when first I felt that felt hat's felt

If a dog chews shoes, whose shoes does he choose?

Nine nice night nurses nursing nicely nightly

**Time to think, reflect and to record your findings here:**

**Your plan of action:**

1. What have you learned from completing this chapter?

2. What are you going to do next to improve/better yourself?

3. Is what you want to achieve realistic, and within your scope or abilities/capabilities?

4. How would you know if you were successful in achieving it?

"Communication is a skill that you can learn. It's like riding a bicycle or typing. If you're willing to work at it, you can rapidly improve the quality of every part of your life."

**Brian Tracy**

# The 4th C
## Is for
# Control

**Influence: Direct: Master**

**Your own personal sense of responsibility**

> "We are the creative force of our life, and through our own decisions rather than our conditions, if we carefully learn to do certain things, we can accomplish these goals".
>
> **Stephen Covey**

### Aims

The aim of this chapter is for you to have more of an understanding of what your personal sense of responsibility is.

### Objectives

The objective is for you to read the chapter and complete the given exercises to help you understand where your internal and external beliefs sit, that is helping to maintain your personality sense of responsibility to face adversity, setbacks, and difficulties in life.

**Let us reflect on what you want to achieve from this chapter here:**

**Personal Responsibility or Individual Responsibility is the idea that human beings choose, instigate, or otherwise cause their own actions. A corollary idea is that because we cause our actions, we can be held morally accountable or legally liable.**

Like they say, life is full of choices and what you make of those choices determines your entire life. And it is these outcomes that determine your job, career, business, the relationships you have (both professional and personal) and your financial situation. These are all a product of those choices you made.

So, in a way, you do have the whole world in your hands through the choices and actions that you choose to make and take.

Having a personal sense of responsibility means being fully accountable for what we think, say, and do in our lives through those choices. This is achieved by working continuously on our own character, recognising your own strengths and weaknesses, and by working on developing your existing skills, knowledge, and experiences to constantly grow, develop and thrive in life.

## Time to read

This is one of the most moving and profound pieces of metaphoric writing I have ever read - and wanted to share it with you. I hope you enjoy it as much as I do.

**There is a hole in the sidewalk – An Autobiography in Five Short Chapters** written by Portia Nelson

**Chapter One. I walk down the street. There's a deep hole in the sidewalk. I fall in. I am lost, I am helpless, it isn't my fault and it takes me forever to find a way out.**

**Chapter Two. I walk down the same street. There's a deep hole in the sidewalk. I pretend I don't see it, I fall in again. I can't believe I'm in the same place, but it isn't my fault and it still takes me a long time to get out.**

**Chapter Three. I walk down the same street. There's a deep hole in the sidewalk. I see it there, I still fall in, it's a habit. My eyes are open, I know where I am, it is my fault and I get out immediately.**

**Chapter Four. I walk down the same street. There's a deep hole in the sidewalk. I walk around it.**

**Chapter Five. I walk down another street.**

## The Locus of Control (LoC)

The Locus of Control is a very powerful piece of psychology that was created by the American psychologist in the 1950s called Julian B. Rotter. Rotter was well known for his work in personality psychology, by moving away from the realms of biological and instinct-driver (habits and actions we are born with) theories of Freudian style psychoanalysis. Instead, Rotter concentrated on developing, growing, and utilising influential social, behavioural, and habitual theories into his work. And it was through this area of study that in 1954, Rotter developed the concept of the Locus of Control.

What this means in layman's terms - or plain language

Rotter believed that our behaviours are not a set of automatic, biological, or instinct based drivers, actions, reactions, or behaviours that we are born with (nature). But we have all developed several habits (shown as actions, reactions, or behaviours) that we have learned through our own unique and individual life experiences from our childhoods, our upbringing, and past experiences (nurture). And what we do is we bring these to our current situation and how we live our lives right now.

It is these habitual actions, reactions and behaviours that we exhibit in response to external stimuli. We respond and recognise these in our own distinct and unique way.

As we found from previous chapters, the mind/brain likes familiarity and seeks what it perceives as logical solutions to getting that familiarity. But as we have also found before in previous chapters. A habitual response may not necessarily be reflecting a genuine, helpful, or beneficial reality. Also, it may not be the best, logical, objective or realistic action or response at times. Rather it is just an inner and outer reflection of learned beliefs, behaviours, actions, and reactions to the current situation. All this creates a habitual response.

So, let us now look more at the Locus of Control. Starting at the beginning, it ties in with Rotter's personality typing, social, behavioural, and habit theories.

The word **Locus** comes from the plural of the Latin **Loci**, for a person's place or location. The Locus of Control (LoC) means that a person's **Place or Locus,** is a **Mental Notion** or **Perception of Control**. This is either 'located' outside their control or inside their control. Which of the two, is dependent on the person's current thinking. So, what we are saying is the control element comes from how much personal control, power or influence a person **believes** they have over events in their life, on both a practical and emotional level.

The main concept behind the Locus of Control is a person's own personal belief about how much sense of personal power and responsibility they have. In how they deal with uncertainty, adversity, and unpredictability and setbacks in life.

So, let us have a look at these two belief systems and ways of thinking in more detail.

## Internal Belief System (Internals)

The person with an Internal Belief System, those Rotter called 'Internals', are the ones who can easily bounce back from adversity, setbacks, making mistakes and failure. As they hold a very strong belief, that whatever life throws at them, they can deal or cope with it, on a practical, mental, and emotional level.

The core belief with an Internal is that they are in control of their lives to a certain extent, and that they can inwardly and outwardly control things to a certain extent. But they are also realists and accept and acknowledge that there is always going to be a certain amount of uncertainty, uncontrollability, unpredictability, failure, and unfairness in their lives one way or another. But with the Internal, they always believe there is always going to be something they can do to take charge, control, or change the situation to a certain degree. Even if it is just changing the way they think, feel, or react about it.

What I have found is the key factor in being an Internal, is the unwavering belief is that they can **cope** with **any** situation on a mental, emotional, and practical level. They may not like it (the situation or the outcome), but they can tolerate it!

## People with an Internal Locus of Control

- Are more likely to take responsibility for their actions
- Tend to be less influenced by the opinions of others
- Often do better at tasks when allowed to work at their own pace
- Usually have a strong sense of self-belief
- Tend to work hard to get the things they want
- Feel confident in the face of adversary
- Can overcome challenges
- Tend to be physically healthier
- Often achieves greater success in life
- Are often more independent
- Accept failure as a part of life
- Are not worried about making mistakes
- Accept themselves for who they are

**What do you recognise in yourself from an Internal Locus of Control perspective?**

## External Belief Systems (Externals)

The opposite to the Internal is what Rotter termed the 'Externals'. The Externals are the ones who find it very difficult to bounce back from any kind of adversity, setback, or failure. And finds it very difficult to tolerate making any kind of mistake. Or being perceived as less than perfect. The Externals are the ones who typically say in the time of adversity or a setback: "Poor old me – It always happens to me, because of X, Y or Z". They are so used to blaming external factors for their current situation.

This unhelpful and limiting thinking further fuels the belief that they are powerless, useless, weak, inadequate, and are not good enough, by constantly being reinforced through habit and repetition. It then becomes a "normal" pattern of thought and behaviour, which then becomes a self-fulfilling prophecy. Thus, the Externals really do believe they have no say, no power, no sway, or no influence over their lives. Because of this, the Externals tend to take no responsibility for anything, and blame everyone or everything for what is going on. Nothing is ever their fault, nothing changes and therefore the cycle of dysfunction is maintained.

To sum it up, the Externals are the ones who tend to believe they are powerless to change or control anything and feel hopeless at the prospect. Because they have so little belief in themselves, their abilities, and capabilities. Their lives tend to be controlled or influenced by outside factors, such as fate, luck, chance or superstition or religion, or by people of significance, power, or authority.

# People with an External Locus of Control

- Blame outside forces for their circumstances
- Often credit fate, luck, or chance for any successes
- Are often very superstitious
- Don't believe that they can change their situation through their own efforts
- Believe others control their lives
- Frequently feel hopeless or powerless in the face of difficult situations
- Are more prone to experiencing learned helplessness
- Afraid to take risk
- Tend to put lower effort put into anything
- Believe that life is random and that they have no control over their life
- Worry about failing
- Worry about making mistakes
- Believe their lives are pre-ordained
- Don't trust themselves
- Don't know who they are
- Not self-accepting
- Believe they are not good enough
- Scared of life

**What do you recognise in yourself from an External Locus of Control perspective?**

## Looking more at external factors

- A belief in luck; of being lucky or unlucky
- A belief that chance events are those over which we have no control
- Aversion or avoidance of taking risk; always playing it safe
- Superstition
- A belief in fate, destiny, or that your life is "mapped out" for you and pre-ordained
- A belief in horoscopes, tarot cards and fortune tellers
- A belief in the paranormal, ghosts, mediums, clairvoyants, and psychics
- A belief in UFOs, Aliens, or Extra-Terrestrials
- Highly religious or with a belief in a higher power or force
- A belief that powerful other people determine the course of your life
- A lack of belief in your own abilities and capabilities
- A lack of belief you can take charge or take control of your life
- Over-protective parents or primary caregivers
- Being manipulated by others
- Illness or ill health
- Living through a time of uncertainty, instability, or unpredictability

---

**What external factors do you recognise in yourself?**

## The Little Boy and Fortune

A little boy wearied with a long journey, lay down overcome with fatigue on the very brink of a deep well. Being within an inch of falling into the water, Dame Fortune, it is said, appeared to him, and waking him from his slumber, thus addressed him: "Little boy, pray wake up: for had you fallen into the well, the blame will be thrown on me, and I shall get an ill name among mortals; for I find that men are sure to blame their calamities to me, however much by their own folly they have really brought them on themselves."

The moral of the story is everyone is more or less a master of his or her own fate.

*From Aesop's Fables*

# The Locus of Control Quiz

The Locus of Control quiz is the driving force in helping you to learn how to develop your personal sense of power, and to become much more powerful and in control of your thoughts, thinking, feeling and emotions and to feel less helpless, less out of control. And believing that you are unable to cope. This is achieved through a set of 30 specially-designed questions that measures your current thinking and beliefs in how much personal power you currently have.

The Locus of Control Quiz here is based loosely on the original **I-E Scale** quiz of 1966.

The Quiz will give you a general idea of where you stand on the Locus of Control scale as an either more of an Internal or External thinker or believer.

The most important thing to remember is that that the Locus of Control Quiz **is not** based on reality. It is a current snapshot on what you currently think and believe about your beliefs, relating to the questions at this present moment in time. There are no right or wrong answers to the quiz. All you are doing is recognising those tiny bits of externality that are currently believing, this is a contributory factor in making you feel powerless, hopeless, and believing you can't cope and feel out of control.

These are the aspects that are fuelling your lack of confidence and lack of self-belief. By recognising them, you can start to challenge, change, or get rid of them!

You may find you are more internal or external in either your work/professional life as opposed to your private/personal life or vice versa.

Please answer each question honestly and truthfully as either an **AGREE** or **DISAGREE** - there is no sitting on the fence with this quiz!

## Exercise Three

## The Locus of Control Quiz

| 1 | I believe it is down to me to get what I want out of life | A | D |
|---|---|---|---|
| 2 | I always say things like "touch wood", "fingers crossed" or "good luck" | A | D |
| 3 | I believe some people are just born lucky | A | D |
| 4 | I believe in ghosts, spirits, and the after-life | A | D |
| 5 | I believe my life is mapped out and is controlled by fate and destiny | A | D |
| 6 | I believe that if I don't succeed on a task first time, then I consider myself to be a failure | A | D |
| 7 | I believe my personality is fixed, so therefore cannot be changed. | A | D |
| 8 | I believe the only ever way I am going to be rich, is if I win the lottery, inherit a fortune, or by a stroke of good luck | A | D |
| 9 | I believe my life is still strongly influenced by my childhood experiences | A | D |
| 10 | I believe the success I have achieved in life, is largely down to a matter of good luck, knowing the right people, or being in the right place at the right time | A | D |
| 11 | I sometimes pray in time of need, or when I need guidance, inspiration, or intervention | A | D |
| 12 | I believe casting my vote in an election can change things, so I always vote | A | D |
| 13 | I have a lucky or unlucky number | A | D |
| 14 | I feel comfortable challenging people in authority | A | D |
| 15 | I believe persistence and hard work is the only way to achieving success | A | D |

| 16 | I believe that the dark, cold winter months can make me feel down and depressed | A | D |
|----|---|---|---|
| 17 | I believe my life is strongly influenced by what other people think of me | A | D |
| 18 | I always salute magpies, won't walk under a ladder, won't cross people on the stairs or put new shoes on a table | A | D |
| 19 | I will never try anything that I am not sure of. In case I fail, cannot do it, get stuck, or not understand the question | A | D |
| 20 | I sometimes read my horoscope in a newspaper or magazine, even though I might not necessary believe what it says | A | D |
| 21 | When other people criticise me, or put me on the spot, it makes me feel unconfident, stressed, and anxious | A | D |
| 22 | My life is strongly influenced by a God, Deity, Higher Being or Power of some kind | A | D |
| 23 | I believe that if people want to do well in life, it doesn't matter what school, college, university, or other educational institution they go to. As they will succeed anyway | A | D |
| 24 | I am always worrying about getting seriously ill or dying | A | D |
| 25 | I believe I am too old to change | A | D |
| 26 | I believe some people have an addictive personality | A | D |
| 27 | I believe that if I really wanted to run a marathon, do an assault course, or climb a mountain, I could do so | A | D |
| 28 | I believe I can get rich by working hard and taking risks | A | D |
| 29 | I believe in life after death | A | D |
| 30 | I don't like to argue or disagree with people, even if I think I am right | A | D |

## Getting your score:

Below is a table of scores from the Locus of Control Quiz.

Each of the 30 questions above has been allocated either a 0 point-score or a 1-point score, dependant on how you personally **AGREED (A)** or **DISAGREED (D)** with the corresponding questions.

The table below shows just the 1-point scores to all 30 questions.

To find out your total overall score, find the corresponding question (QUES:) to the answer (ANS:) you have recorded as an AGREE (A) or DISAGREE (D).

Give yourself 1-point if the answer you have given matches the answer in table below.

Once you have tallied up all your points, and have a Grand Total, then you can see if you are more Internal or External with your current beliefs and thinking.

| QUES: | ANS: | QUES: | ANS: | QUES: | ANS: | QUES: | ANS: | QUES: | ANS: | |
|---|---|---|---|---|---|---|---|---|---|---|
| 1 | D | 7 | A | 13 | A | 19 | A | 25 | A | |
| 2 | A | 8 | A | 14 | D | 20 | A | 26 | A | |
| 3 | A | 9 | A | 15 | D | 21 | A | 27 | D | |
| 4 | A | 10 | A | 16 | A | 22 | A | 28 | D | |
| 5 | A | 11 | A | 17 | A | 23 | D | 29 | A | |
| 6 | A | 12 | D | 18 | A | 24 | A | 30 | A | GRAND TOTAL |
| = | / 6 | = | /6 | = | /6 | = | / 6 | = | / 6 | = / 30 |

Please write your total score here: ......../...**30**....

If you scored between 0 – 5, you are very INTERNAL, and have a very low EXTERNAL Locus of Control.

If you scored between 6 – 10, you are INTERNAL, and is only edging towards having an EXTERNAL Locus of Control in certain areas in your life.

If you scored between 11 – 15, you are moderately INTERNAL, and are certainly edging towards having more of an EXTERNAL Locus of Control in certain areas in your life.

If you scored between 16 - 25, then you are very EXTERNAL, and have a very low INTERNAL Locus of Control.

If you scored between 25 - 30, then you are extremely EXTERNAL, and have either a very low or no INTERNAL Locus of Control.

**Exercise Four**

## Lessons Learned

I would like you to reflect on the questions you scored a point on, alongside the lists of tendencies in their various contexts, and jot down what you have learned here.

**What do you recognise in yourself from the LoC Quiz?**

**Exercise Five**

Here are five further questions for you to think about and answer relating to your current Locus of Control quiz answers.

1. What are the implications of my LOC score in my life right now?

2. Does my LOC score ring true to me, given the Internal and External tendencies listed above?

3. How does my LOC affect my ability to succeed?

4. What kind of LOC score would have been better?

5. Did you recognise any patterns or themes in your results?

Below are some more in-depth, thought-provoking questions that can help you to find the answers you are looking for.

Below are some more in-depth, thought-provoking questions that can help you to find the answers you are looking for.

To work towards having more of an Internal Locus of Control.

- Where does this belief come from?

- How long have I had this belief?

- Is the belief based on fact?

- What real evidence do I have to support this belief?

- Is the belief I am holding onto "just a nice thought", or comforting me in some way?

- Why am I still choosing to hold onto, or maintain this belief?

- Does this belief come from another person?

- If yes, who is that person?

- Why is it such a powerful belief?

- Would other people think it was odd, strange, or peculiar if you didn't have this belief?

- Would I feel left out if I didn't have this belief?

- What would happen if I got rid of this belief?

- How different would my life be?

- Do I have any physical, mental, or emotional needs to hold onto, or maintain this belief?

- What is stopping me getting rid of this belief?

> "It is our choices that show what we truly are,
> far more than our abilities."
>
> J. K. Rowling

**Your plan of action:**

1. What have you learned from completing this chapter?

2. What are you going to do next to improve/better yourself?

3. Is what you want to achieve realistic, and within your scope or abilities/capabilities?

4. How would you know if you were successful in achieving it?

# To sum up …

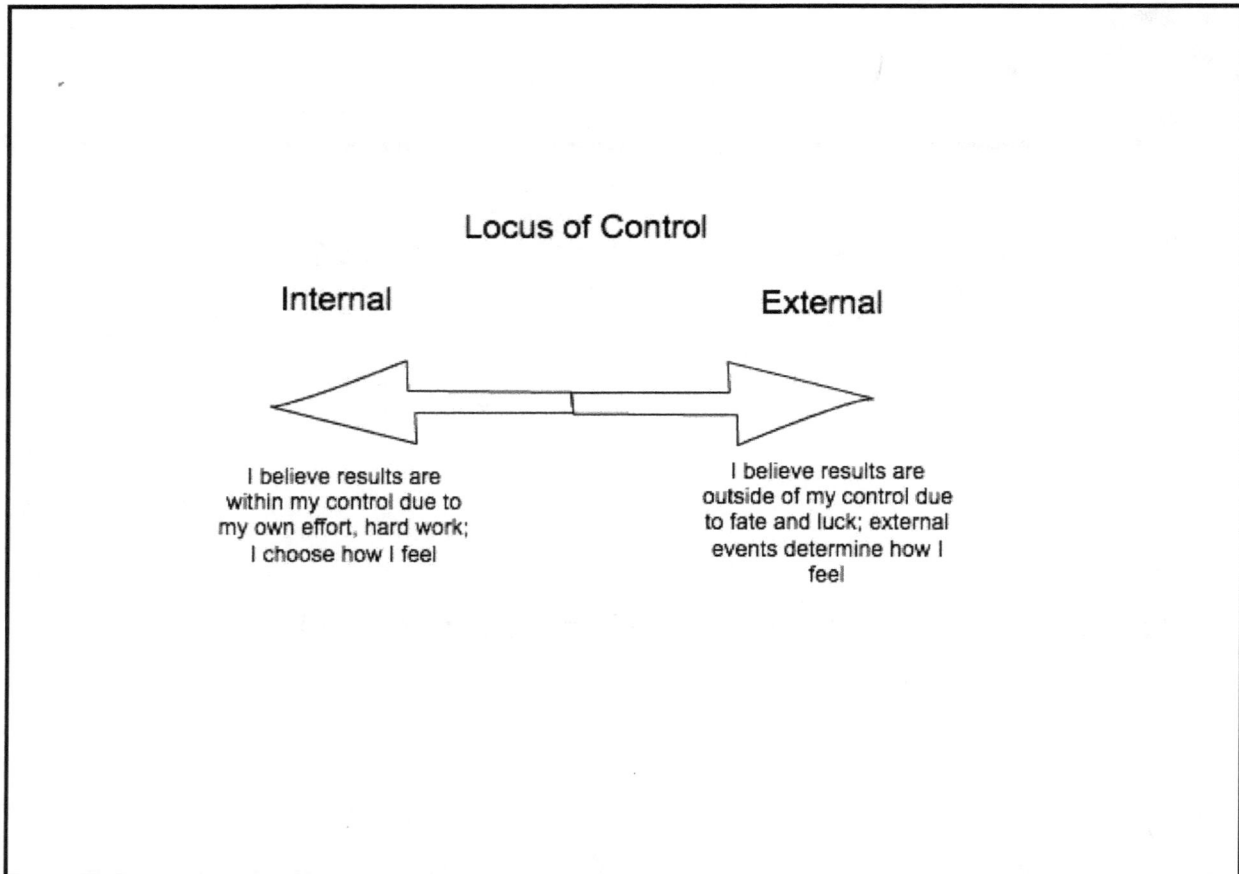

## Inspiration Time

Please find below, an inspiration piece, that was written by Julie Futcher, who owns and manages her highly successful company – The Sales Manager. This piece reflects her hard work, determination, motivation, and positive thinking, that has gotten her to where she is today.

"I have never been academic! I left full-time education at 18 with two 'O' levels and a secretarial diploma and started my working life as a secretary. If I had said to my 18-year-old self that one day I would be running a successful business of my own, I wouldn't have believed you.

Back then, non-academic people were not given the encouragement, especially in schools, to believe that you *can* achieve your dreams.

So how did I get where I am today? Having become very disillusioned with being a secretary (I worked for a boss that was a bit of a tyrant), I made the decision to enter a sales role. I realised very quickly, that your success is not governed by a qualification or a diploma, it is about what you do and your attitude.

I worked hard, I learnt and very quickly I became successful; these values have stayed with me.

This book will help you to understand that you *can* achieve your dreams. It will equip you with the belief and the skills that you need to help you through life. Read, learn, embrace and enjoy".

**Julie Futcher – Managing Director**

**The Sales Manager -** www.thesales-manager.co.uk

# The 5th C
## Is for
# Character

**Personality: Nature: Individuality**

# Who Am I?

> "The brain is behind the really big questions we have. Who am I, what is my identity? What is that based on? If memories are encoded in connectomes, your personality might be in your connectome. If that's the case, that's the basis of your uniqueness as a person".
>
> **Sebastian Seung**

## Aims

The aim of this chapter is for you to have more of an understanding of you and your personality, and how it all comes together in making you the person you are.

## Objectives

The objective is for you to read the chapter and complete the given exercises to help change the way you think, feel, and view yourself. How? By getting you to examine your personality in greater detail. Then you can highlight those facets you want to change about yourself, and keep on improving those positive, helpful, and beneficial parts of you.

**Let us reflect on what you want to achieve from this chapter here:**

# Personality

There are two explanations to where the word personality stems from.

The first explanation derives from the Greek *Persona* – which means Mask. So therefore, the study of a person's personality is the study of the masks that people wear. These masks are the personas that people project and display, but also include the inner parts of psychological experience which we collectively call our self.

The second explanation comes from the Latin word *Personalitas*, which comes from the word *Personalis*, meaning personal, derived from the word *persona*, meaning person.

I will leave you to make you own mind up to which one you agree with!

**So, what is your personality?**

Throughout the ages, man has always been fascinated about who we are, what is the self. The true "I". The person deep inside us, who makes us the person who we are.

Our personality is created through a combination of two factors:

1. **Nature – What we are born with**
2. **Nurture – What we have learned**

Those from nature comprise of those aspects of our personality that are an integral part of us, and most often cannot be changed, (but they can be modified or softened and played down slightly). For example, if you are a quiet, shy, and private person, you are not going to suddenly be the life and soul of the party, wearing your heart on your sleeve, with everyone suddenly becoming your new best friend. However, you may become more accepting of yourself; not so quiet or shy and a bit more open and honest through practice and perseverance.

Listed below are those factors that make up the nature side of your personality.

- Genes
- Inherited traits
- Intelligence/Intellect

The other factor, those nurturing aspects of our personality come from external factors that have enabled us to learn (normally in early childhood). Where we have created a belief system around those external factors. Which we looked at earlier in the book.

Listed below are those factors that make up the nurturing side of your personality.

- Who you were brought up by (parents, primary caregivers etc)
- Environmental factors (such as how and where we were brought up)
- Culture
- Social Class/Socio-Economic Group
- Religion
- Early childhood experiences (formative years 0 - 6 years old)
- Young childhood experiences (6 – 10 years old)
- Teen-age experiences (13 – 19 years old)
- Adolescence / Young People experiences (10 – 24 years old)

So, we now know that our personality is a combination of both nature and nurture and can be altered by changing the way you think, feel and act, react or behave in certain situations.

**Exercise One**

## The "I am" exercise

Without over-analysing the following exercise. I want you to write down **10 honest** endings to the "I am . . ." statements below. Those statements that you think, feel, or believe about yourself, that automatically spring to mind in, and **NOT** what you want to be or think you should be.

**Give yourself 3 MINUTES to complete this exercise.**

| 1 | I am … | |
|---|--------|---|
| 2 | I am … | |
| 3 | I am … | |
| 4 | I am … | |
| 5 | I am … | |
| 6 | I am … | |
| 7 | I am … | |
| 8 | I am … | |
| 9 | I am … | |
| 10 | I am … | |

Do you think these statements sum up your personality?

Why or why not?

The idea behind this exercise is that it is suggested that we get a good idea of what personality is by listening to what we say when we use "I".

When you say "I", you are, in effect, summing up everything about yourself: your likes and dislikes, fears and virtues, strengths and weaknesses.

**"I don't want other people to decide who I am.
I want to decide that for myself".
Emma Watson**

**Time to think, reflect and to record your findings here:**

## Something for you to read

I found this online whilst researching this book, and found the questions very thought-provoking, and thought it gave great perspective on the question of – "Who am I?"

**Christopher Titmuss**
**Dharma Blog**
**A Buddhist Perspective**

## Who am I?

There are avenues to approach this question.

Am I my name, my roles, mind, and body? There can be sudden or gradual changes in these areas.

Am I always the same? If so, there is nothing I can do to change myself?

If I am always changing, then my self in the past, is not the same as the one in the present.

So, I cannot be held responsible for what happened to my old selves in the past.

If one part of me always stays the same and one part of me always changes, then what part stays the same and what part changes?

# WHO AM I?

A short and reflective poem by Christopher Titmuss

I just want to know who I am
where I am, what I truly am
and what I exist for at all.
I want to know what is named 'me,'

Who am I? Also, who are you?
Am I in the world? Am I one with it?
Separate from the world or not?
Or am out of this world or not?
I feel so connected with all around
But sometimes I just don't feel involved
and feel quite detached from this world.

I am not who you think I am.
I claim I am not the same self,
I would love to know my true self,
be sure of who I am to myself.
"This is my true self, my real self,
my steadfast self, my only self,
independent self, the real me."

Who will now point out this true self to me?
Is it another self in me given this task?
Can I point out my true self to myself?

I claim I am not the same self,
as I remember as a child long ago.
I claim I am different from this self from the past.
If so, then I can take no praise nor blame
for what I did or didn't do in the past.
After all, myself today is not same
as the self who had acted yesterday.

Why should one self in me judge part of me?
Why should one part of me give
another part of me a hard time?

Why do that if I am always the same person?
Why do that if I am always changing?

If myself is just the same self every day,
yesterday, tomorrow and now,
that means that I always remain the same;
events then make no difference to myself,
nothing at all can affect me.

If I am really changing from day to day
then nothing can affect me
for more than a moment
because I am different
now from what I was just before.
Yesterday's self bears no significance today.
My old self sometimes says nothing about today
Yet my old self sometimes dominates today.
My old self sometimes shadows over today.

Why should my old self judge today's self
if I am changing every day?
Why should my old self judge today's self
if I am the same self every day?

Do I consist of lots of different selves?
Tell me which one of my many selves
do I rely upon.

If I always remain the same, then
no chance for any kind of change;
I can't develop or regress.
It would not matter what I did,
what I am doing or what I will do.

I cannot find a true self to pinpoint.
Which self within points out the true self?
Can I rely upon the self that points out the true self?
So, there is no self-assurance here
True self, changing self, different selves?
This all seems rather inconsequential.

Then I like to think I am both,
a true unchanging self and a changing self.

Which bit of me shows my true self?
Which bit of me shows my changing self?
What connects up these two kinds of selves?
True self, changing self, different selves,
old self, new self, synthesis?

Reality refutes every thesis.

Such a relief ….

Christopher says "In my book of poetry, *Poems from the Edge*, I explored these themes. The title of this poem is Who am I? It is available from: https://www.christophertitmussblog.org/who-am-i-a-short-reflection-and-poem

**Time to think, reflect and to record your findings here:**

## Personality Types

In my professional life, I have found people are absolutely fascinated about personality typing. And If you search "personality types" on the internet, then there are various models of on-line tests you can take, to determine what is deemed your very own personality type.

Listed below are the most popular ones.

- Myers – Briggs Type Indicator (MBTI)
- Psycho-Analysis
- Holland Codes
- DISC Assessment
- The Winslow Personality Profile
- The Holtzman Inkblot Technique
- The Hexaco Personality Inventory

So, what exactly is a personality type? Even though most of us fancy ourselves to be truly unique individuals in our own right. There is a part in all of us, that wants physical, mental, emotional, and social connection with our fellow man (or woman!). We want to have connectivity, so that the people around us can understand who we are, what we want, and how we can get it, and vice-versa.

What psychologists and behaviourists (people who study human behaviour) have spent years studying and researching, are those similar patterns in our personalities that we all exhibit. And it is in these patterns of thought and behaviours that suggest we all share some very similar qualities, traits, and tendencies regardless of whether we like it or not. However, it does not mean that if someone else has the same personality type as you, they will think, act, or behave in the exact same way as you would do.

But, why not? Because every single person is truly unique and special in their own way. This is because we have all lived our own lives through our own eyes. And it would be truly impossible to replicate anyone else's thoughts, feelings, emotions, reactions, and patterns of behaviour 100%. Plus, we all have our own individual likes, dislikes, preferences, and preferred choices. This is alongside our own little quirks, idiosyncrasies, and personal modes of behaviour and the way we react to things. It is all these contributory factors that make us an individual human being. If we didn't have these unique factors that pertain just to us. Then we would be like little robots. And be a carbon copy of everyone else around us. Think of the film, **Stepford Wives**!

# Determining Personality Types

So, what determines what is a personality type? Psychologists have found there are five main factors that determine different personality types. The big five factors are:

- Openness. People who are open like learning new things and enjoying new experiences. They have a wide variety of hobbies, interests, passions, or pursuits. Traits includes being open, honest, and frank.
- Conscientiousness. People that have a high degree of conscientiousness are the ones who are conscientious, reliable, and prompt. Traits include being organised, methodical, and thorough.
- Extraversion. People who are extraverts get their energy from interacting with others. While introverts get their energy from within themselves, extraversion includes the traits of being energetic, talkative, and assertive.
- Agreeableness. People who are agreeable are those individuals who are warm, friendly, cooperative, and compassionate. People with low agreeableness may be more cold, distant, private, and reserved. Traits include being kind, affectionate, and sympathetic.
- Neuroticism. This factor relates to one's emotional stability and degree of negative emotions. People that score high on neuroticism experience emotional instability and negative emotions. Traits include being moody, tense and paranoid.

However, the only problem with personalities is that most people tend to think that their personality is "fixed", "rigid" or "unchangeable". That they cannot change it, as it is what they were born with. Yes, a certain part of that statement may be true. For example, someone who is quiet by nature isn't going to suddenly be the life and soul of the party. But they can learn to become more confident in themselves, speak more with authority and put their point of view across in an easy, relaxed, and gentle manner, while remaining true to their nature.

So, why is understanding ourselves and our personality type so important to our mental, emotional, psychological, physical, and spiritual health? The better we understand ourselves and others, and the reasons why we think, feel, act, or behave in certain situations, then the more successful we are going to be in those situations, whenever they arise. So therefore, life is going to be far more pleasant and easier. And certainly, more calm, relaxed, and stress-free. When we understand ourselves better, we tend to have happier relationships, be healthier, earn more money and more productive in our work, job, or career.

Now, I am not saying that understanding your personality is panacea which can make your life perfect. Like we said previously, there are certain elements of your personality you can change, if you really wanted to. But there is always going to be some aspect that can't be changed. There are always going to be people in your life who push your buttons, irritate the life out of you, or piss you off. There will always be situations that you do not like, don't want to be in, or cannot control. But I do genuinely believe that taking a good, long deep look at yourself and your personality is one way of getting to know the real you. You can then be a lot more honest and self-accepting of yourself. This relies on total honesty on your part, and maybe facing up to some uncomfortable truths and realisations! But don't forget, we are just looking at those unhelpful, negative, and limiting parts that are holding us back or are contributing to your problem, and stopping you living the life you want to live!

How you choose to work within your personality is entirely up to you. It is all down to you taking responsibility for the actions you take and the decisions you make. Either you are a patient person, or not. A responsible person or not. The only way to change your personality is to become aware of those parts of your personality you do not like, those which are not helpful, useful, or beneficial or no longer serve any kind of purpose. Then take active steps to become the person you want to be.

## Exercise Two

**Taking time to have a good look inside of yourself**

I would like you to think about the big five factors above that determine different personality types. And for you to record below **THREE** positive/negative, helpful/unhelpful aspects of your personality that you recognise in yourself within those big five factors.

## 1. Openness
   1.
   2.
   3.

## 2. Conscientiousness
   1.
   2.
   3.

## 3. Extraversion
   1.
   2.
   3.

## 4. Agreeableness
   1.
   2.
   3.

## 5. Neuroticism
   1.
   2.
   3.

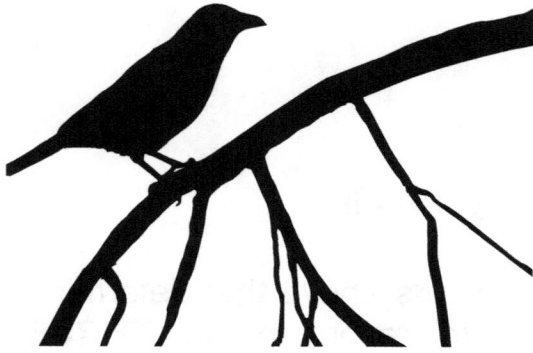

## The Crow and the Raven

A Crow was jealous of the Raven, because he was considered a bird of good omen and always attracted the attention of men, who noted by his flight the good or evil course of future events.

Seeing some travellers approaching, the Crow flew up into a tree, and perching herself on one of the branches, cawed as loudly as she could. The travellers turned towards the sound and wondered what it foreboded, when one of them said to his companion: "Let us proceed on our journey, my friend, for it is only the caw of a crow, and her cry, you know, is no omen."

The morale of the story is those who assume a character which does not belong to them, only make themselves ridiculous.

*From Aesop's Fables*

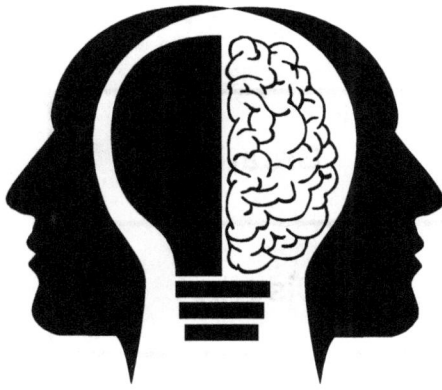

## Personality Traits

The word *trait* comes from the Latin *tractus* – meaning drawing, dragging, and pulling. In the late 15th century, in Middle French, trait meant a line, stroke, or feature. In 1752, trait: a sense of "particular feature, distinguishing quality" was first recorded in English. And that it is the meaning/definition that we still use today.

So, what is a personality trait? A personality trait reflects a person's characteristic patterns of thoughts, feelings, emotional responses, and behaviours that can be defined as:

- Actions
- Attitudes
- Behaviours

These three personality traits can either be classed a positive or negative trait. And can give a very good indicator to if a person is living a happy, balanced, relaxed, and fulfilled life.

**Below are some examples of some positive personality traits:**

- Being honest no matter what the situation is
- Taking responsibility for your actions
- Admitting when you have made a mistake, and learning from it
- Being adaptable, flexible, and dependable where it counts
- Having the drive to keep going no matter what
- Having compassion and understanding
- Being patient
- Getting up the courage to do what's right in those tough situations
- Being loyal to your friends and loved ones

# Here's a few more to consider:

| | | |
|---|---|---|
| Adventurous | Affable | Creative |
| Cultured | Dependable | Discreet |
| Encouraging | Reliable | Exuberant |
| Fair | Fearless | Observant |
| Helpful | Humble | Suave |
| Imaginative | Meticulous | Obedient |
| Impartial | Independent | Optimistic |
| Intelligent | Keen | Gregarious |
| Persistent | Capable | Charming |
| Precise | Confident | Dutiful |
| Trusting | Valiant | Harmonious |

**Below are some examples of Negative Personality Traits**

- Takes no responsibility
- Blames others
- Is never your fault
- Never learns from past mistakes
- Often credits fate, luck, or chance for any successes
- Does not believe that they can change their situation through their own efforts
- Worries about failing
- Worries about making mistakes
- Being rigid, unadaptable, and uncompromising
- Gives up without a fight
- Unreliable and lets people down
- Impatient and inconsiderate to other people's needs
- Always worrying about the "what if" scenario

# Here are a few more negative traits to consider:

| Laziness | Picky | Sullen |
|---|---|---|
| Pompous | Dishonest | Finicky |
| Sarcastic | Arrogant | Cowardly |
| Sneaky | Rude | Quarrelsome |
| Impulsive | Slovenly | Self-centred |
| Boorish | Surly | Unfriendly |
| Unruly | Thoughtless | Stingy |
| Bossy | Vulgar | Malicious |
| Conceited | Obnoxious | Selfish |

A whole host of other bad characteristics can also be considered personality traits if you practise these things habitually.

# Exercise Three

## The good, the bad and the ugly

I would like you to think about the positive and negative personality traits that you recognise in yourself – or that others have said about you. And for you to record your findings in the table below.

| Positive/Helpful Personality Traits | Negative/Unhelpful Personality Traits |
|---|---|
|  |  |
|  |  |
|  |  |
|  |  |
|  |  |
|  |  |
|  |  |
|  |  |
|  |  |
|  |  |

**Time to think, reflect and to record your findings here:**

**Exercise Four**

**Listed below are five inspirational quotes around personality. Which one is your favourite, and why?**

1. "Always be yourself, express yourself, have faith in yourself, do not go out and look for a successful personality and duplicate it".
Bruce Lee

2. "There is an amazing power getting to know your inner self and learning how to use it and not fight with the world. If you know what makes you happy, your personality, interests, and capabilities, just use them, and everything else flows beautifully".
Juhi Chawla

3. "We are all born with a unique genetic blueprint, which lays out the basic characteristics of our personality as well as our physical health and appearance . . . And yet, we all know that life experiences do change us".
Joan D. Vinge

4. "The 'self-image' is the key to human personality and human behavior. Change the self-image and you change the personality and the behavior".
Maxwell Maltz

5. "We recruit our people for personality. We look for the people person, with innate warmth, sweetness, and intelligence. These are the people who are sending your message out to the customers and potential customers, so we recruit for personality first and foremost"
Steve Wynn

**Time to think, reflect and to record your findings here:**

## The FOUR Personality Types

And now to the exciting part of the chapter. Looking at the **FOUR** Personality Types, and to see what you can identify in yourself.

The methodology I use is the one is based on a combination of traditional psychoanalysis, The Holland Codes and Colour Psychology. So, why do I use these three models? Because I believe they all give a realistic appraisal of you as the whole person, that is a true representation of yourself. I have tried to write it in a fun, relaxed and easy to understand way that you can identify with and start to work on.

To achieve this, I have designed this chapter for you to look at both your strengths and weaknesses, and for you to assess both the positive/helpful and negative/unhelpful sides of your personality, and your personality type. Thus, helping you to make more of an informed decision, based on fact and logic, rather than just on emotion alone. This will help you get past old ways of thinking such as: 'I should, must and ought to be that type', or 'people in the past have told me I am like this or like that, so it must be true'.

The most important thing to remember is this exercise is not designed to beat yourself up mentally or emotionally. Or to make you feel you are a nasty, horrible or useless person. It is for you to start to identify those unhelpful, unbeneficial, and limiting parts of your personality that are holding you back, and not allowing you to make the very best of your life and what it has to offer.

For a bit of fun, and to stop people getting too hung up on what they think they want to be, or what they believe they should be, or what other people have called them in the past. I have called my 4 Personality Types:

1. **The White Dove**
2. **The Serene Swan**
3. **The Ruling Rooster**
4. **The Proud Peacock**

The reason behind the names will become much clearer when you read the descriptions of the four personality types below.

## Let us start

What I want you to do first, is read the descriptions of all the four personality types below, and then highlight and record the positive parts that resonate with you. Then do the same with the negative, unhelpful, and unbeneficial parts of you; as these are the areas you are going to be working on.

What you will find is when you read the next chapter, where we look at personality types and traits in more detail, you will be able to see more clearly what personality types are more suited to certain types of jobs, careers, and businesses. And life in general!

## The White Dove - The Carer

White Doves are traditionally known as the peacekeepers. They are the symbol of peace, love, purity, and freedom, it still carries the same strong and universal message since it has done since ancient times. And here is another interesting fact. Did you know doves produce their own milk? Yes, it's called "crop milk" or "pigeons milk." It's an oddity in nature for birds to produce their own milk to feed their young. From this unique ability, we can glean the symbolism of nurturing. In fact, doves are also commonly considered a symbol of motherhood.

As people, your White Doves are going to be the loyal, faithful, kind, caring, and nurturing type of people. Just like a child in some ways. This is because they are primarily driven by the need of just wanting to be liked, to be wanted, and thought of as being an all-round nice person. They tend to live in the moment. Wear their hearts on their sleeves. And are driven by emotion. But can in some situations, or to some people, they can come across as being far too emotional, too needy, or just far too nice.

The White Doves are often excellent communicators and can make people feel safe, secure, happy and at ease. They are very often very open, chatty, and friendly, with a sense of openness and honesty about them. Because one of their biggest drivers is to please and to be nice, they are quite laid back as a rule. As they don't want to be seen making a fuss or drama. Or want to give any cause to rock the boat. But to be there unassumingly in the background.  Making sure everything is perfect, by just getting on with the job in hand. And blaming themselves when things go wrong. Perfectionistic tendencies are often seen in White Doves, as they are trying so hard to make life perfect for everyone around them.

One of the biggest characteristics with the White Dove is the tendency to people-please and be nice and kind too much. But, the flipside of being too nice, too kind, and too kind and caring, is that people often take advantage and use the White Doves for all they are worth. And because the White Dove wants to keep the peace, and not rock the boat, they then find it difficult to admit to themselves that it is happening, and to be assertive. Instead, they turn it inwards, and blame themselves, even when they know they are being taken advantage of. Because the White Doves are too busy burying their heads in the sand, blaming themselves and pretending it is not happening, this can go on quite un-noticed for a long time. And it is only when the White Dove starts to feel or notice they are not being appreciated, or that they are being taken advantage of, that problems tend to arise. Because the White Dove always wants to feel good in the moment, they can turn inwards and will start to self-medicate to make themselves feel better. These actions include but are not exclusive to smoking and drinking too much, taking drugs (recreational and prescription), shopping, spending money, watching pornography, over exercising etc. to give themselves that instant gratification of making themselves feel better in the present moment, right now!

Some of the biggest negatives with the White Doves are learned helplessness, subservience, feebleness, feelings of powerlessness, martyrdom alongside a sense of self-pity (the 'poor old me' syndrome). The White Doves are the ones who stay late at work, do things outside of their pay scale, and are often passed over for promotion as they never make a fuss.


Think of the White Dove represented by the colour GREEN. As green represents peace and harmony between nature and nurture, by trying to obtain feelings of balance and equilibrium. Green also represents greed, jealousy, envy and decay.

# Typical traits of the White Dove Personality Type

| | | |
|---|---|---|
| KIND and CARING | LOVING | SOCIABLE |
| SELF-CENTRED | TENDENCY TO SELF–BLAME | EASILY HURT |
| AFFECTED BY OTHER PEOPLE'S EMOTIONS | OVER-SENSITIVE | SENTIMENTAL |
| PEOPLE-PLEASERS | IMAGINATIVE | PERFECTIONISTIC |
| TOLERANT | EMPATHETIC | AN "ALL OR NOTHING" EMOTIONAL REACTION |
| DESIRES INSTANT GRATIFICATION TO FEEL GOOD | EASILY EXPRESSES THE EMOTIONS FELT | WANTS TO FEEL LOVED & HAPPY NOW! |
| WARM | OPEN | FRIENDLY |
| COMPASSIONATE | MARTYR | RELIABLE |
| DAYDREAMERS | SELF PITYING (Poor old me) | HAPPY |
| LEARNED HELPLESSNESS | HONEST | LIKEABLE |

**Time to think, reflect and to record your findings here:**

## The Serene Swan – The Thinker

The Serene Swan is the complete opposite to the White Dove.

The Serene Swan is not driven by emotion; but by power, self-control, and routine. By being in charge, and by being and having total control of themselves and others in a very calm and subtle way. The Serene Swan spends a lot of their life thinking and worrying about their lives, and often defers pleasure to brood, obsess and ruminate on how to carry out their plans and goals, to get the power and control they so desire. Because this personality type has a very high desire for control (being a bit of a control freak), with a real need to be in charge and to be in, or on top of things. They tend to be real thinkers and like to plan everything in minute detail. So much that they tend to be highly demanding perfectionists of themselves, and of others around them. And because of this, they are very obsessive in their very nature. And this can be very stressful and demanding on themselves, and on others who have to live, or work with them. They can literally spend days, weeks, or months brooding, obsessing, and ruminating about the tiniest little detail to get what they want or to control. And because they are such perfectionists, everything must be perfect, so they tend to be very single-minded, driven and determined. This in turn can come across as being very cold, uncaring, ruthless, selfish, secretive, and paranoid.

And like the swan in nature, they like to keep what they are thinking and feeling very well hidden from others. That is not showing any kind of weakness or vulnerability. But what they are doing is paddling like mad under the surface. One prominent characteristic about the Serene Swan is one where people will often say to friends, family or loved ones is that they don't really know anything about you, only what you choose to tell. Or that they can't get a sense of what you are really like as a person, as you never give anything away, as you are so private, reserved and / or shy.

Why? To maintain that perceived cool, calm, collected and controlled exterior. This is one of the main characteristics of the Serene Swan is that they are always working hard to maintain that dignified demeanour of being very calm and in control of themselves, and the situation. So, as you can see, perception of the self and being in control is the name of the game for the Serene Swan.

As a person, the Serene Swan are normally very bright, intelligent, analytical, and logical in their thinking and a lover of routine and order. Quite often they are seen a being quite nerdy, because of their systematic and focused outlook. The Serene Swan is the kind of person who needs to understand the process. Everything to the Serene Swan is well thought-out and executed. And they certainly do not waste time on frivolities, frills, or fancies.

The Serene Swan is focused on achieving the end-result, through goal-setting and planning, by utilising their own drive, determination, tenacity, and own bloody mindedness to get where they want to be.

On the negative side the Serene Swan is constantly brooding, obsessing, and ruminating about the smallest detail, and finds it difficult to relax or switch off. This can make them jealous, suspicious, and paranoid. The Serene Swan is often prone to stress, anxiety, and OCD (Obsessive Compulsive Disorder) because they are desperate to be in control at all times. But saying that, it is not that uncommon for the Serene Swan to be socially awkward and have social anxiety – a fear of being judged/not being good enough, alongside perfectionistic tendencies (wanting everything to be perfect), due to the very obsessive and controlling part of their personality.

Think of the Serene Swan represented by the colour BLUE. As blue represents depth, expansiveness, safety and security. Blue can also represent coldness, aloofness and being rigid, righteous and conservative.

# Typical traits of the SERENE SWAN Personality Type

| | | |
|---|---|---|
| OFFSETS PLEASURE INTO THE FUTURE | DETACHED AND NOT DRIVEN BY EMOTION | IMPORTANT NEEDS ARE SAFETY, SECURITY, HEALTH, MONEY & POWER |
| DRIVEN BY POWER & AUTHORITY | SINGLE-MINDED | MANIPULATIVE |
| BROODS, OBSESSES AND RUMINATES | COMPETITIVE | DETERMINED |
| TENACIOUS | DRIVEN | RUTHLESS |
| CLOSED PEOPLE | NOT SENSITIVE TO OTHER'S EMOTIONS | GOOD DECISION-MAKERS |
| SUSPICIOUS | HIGHLY-ORGANISED | SELF-DISCIPLINED |
| A HIGH DESIRE FOR CONTROL | PERFECTIONIST | LOVES ROUTINE |
| STRONG EGO | METHODICAL | FOCUSED SENSE OF PURPOSE |
| STUBBORN | PERSISTENT | ATTENTION TO DETAIL |
| PARANOID | SELFISH | METHODICAL |

**Time to think, reflect and to record your findings here:**

# The Ruling Rooster – The Warrior

The Ruling Rooster is the warrior type of personality. The Ruling Rooster is the complete opposite to the White Swan in as much as the Ruling Rooster is a natural leader and likes everyone to know that he or she is in charge. This is achieved by leading from the front through strong leadership skills and the strength of their personality, or by intimidation or through sheer brute force to get the desired result. As you can see, the Ruling Rooster is not for the faint-hearted or a force to be reckoned with. You could envisage the Ruling Rooster literally ruling the roost and living by the adage of – it's my way or the highway type of attitude. The Ruling Rooster is not out to make friends, but to get the job in hand done, with the minimum of fuss and whatever tools he or she has at their disposal to get it done.

So, the Ruling Roosters are the power wielders of the world. The go-getters. The visionaries. They are ones who have a strong, dominant personality and every day they burn with the passion and drive to succeed and be the very best that they can be. They love and live an action packed, results-oriented life. And are the ones you see leading from the front at a fast, confident pace. Taking risks and being really, purposeful in what they are saying and doing to achieving their end goal both personally and professionally. And certainly not taking any prisoners along the way!

One thing to note is the Ruling Rooster likes being centre of attention, but for the end goal of what they have done and achieved, and the power it brings. And not for just being centre of attention per se like the Proud Peacock.

However, the Ruling Roosters can be very charming, charismatic. and enigmatic, and very used to getting their own way. So, it is not that uncommon for the Ruling Rooster to display outbursts of anger or displeasure, or even sulk if they don't get their own way! Or even try to bully, intimate, threat or cajole the unwilling participant or party.

Think of the Ruling Rooster represented by the colour RED. As red represents energy, power, passion and determination. It can also represent anger, danger, war, death and destruction.

## Typical traits of the RULING ROOSTER Personality Type

| | | |
|---|---|---|
| RESULTS DRIVEN | DECISIVE | ASSERTIVE |
| CONFIDENT | DETERMINED | DISCIPLINED |
| OBESSIVE | INDEPENDENT | IMPATIENT |
| RUTHLESS | BULLY | INTIMIDATING |
| HARSH | CRITICAL | UN-EMOTIONAL |
| COLD | UNCARING | DETERMINED |
| TENACIOUS | EGOTISTICAL | AGGRESSIVE |
| VIGOROUS | IMPULSIVE | RISK TAKER |
| EXTROVERTED | STRONG LEADER | GO - GETTER |
| ATTENTION SEEKING | COMPETITIVE | INSENSITIVE |

**Time to think, reflect and to record your findings here:**

## The Proud Peacock – The Dramatist

The Proud Peacock is the dramatist type of personality. You can tend to read the Proud Peacock personality type like a book, everything is either physically, emotionally, and linguistically (spoken words/language) dramatic – from their body and verbal language, facial expressions, mode of dress, demeanour, attitudes, reactions, behaviours, and sense of humour. Think of the theatrical, over-the-top, look at my beautiful feathers type of personality. Then think of a strutting peacock showing off their beautiful feathers, and you can see the similarities!

The Proud Peacock type of personality is all about the Proud Peacock, living life as if it is one big central stage, with them strutting around and quite often being the star attraction. So, to the Proud Peacock, everything is about them, and everyone else around is just an audience to play to, sometimes in a very 'in your face' way, or sometimes dramatists can be dramatic in very subtle ways.

Interestingly, you can get people who have social anxiety or are a bit quieter and shyer, be a Proud Peacock. This can manifest itself in your dramatic side being shown when you are with people you know, like, trust and feel comfortable with. Being in a front-of-house/front line job, singing in a choir or band or being involved in amateur dramatics, or even being a storyteller, telling jokes and making people laugh, these are all variables of the Proud Peacock.

It can also be in the way you dress, your shoes, your hair, your make-up, and the jewellery you wear, or even the car you drive (think Porsche or Lamborghini). Everything is shouting: "Look at me".

It can even manifest itself in people being dramatic when they don't get their own way, or when they want to get attention, sympathy, or recognition on practical or emotional level of sort.

So, what happens when the Proud Peacocks do not get the attention, sympathy, adulation or praise they so want and desire, or if things do not go their way. The main factor in all these situations, is the Proud Peacock tends to be quite child-like and immature. Quite often they are prone to either temper tantrums, anger outbursts with lots of stomping of feet, hand waving and facial gestures, throwing things around, kicking/hitting things in anger or frustration. Or they sulk or pout, and turn inwards, and go off in a strop and will not talk to you, but they will make a big show, a big drama of not talking to you. Think of a small child not getting their own way and throwing a tantrum, or not talking and sulking. That is your Proud Peacock.

Because the Proud Peacocks are all about drama, they tend to be good fun, passionate, sociable, outgoing and will be the ones to get the party going. They can also push social norms, with outrageous dress, language, and behaviour. Another trait most Proud Peacocks have is to be 'people's people', in the sense they tend to make people feel very at ease, calm, happy and relaxed, and have the wonderful ability to bring people out of their shells. And because they are so sociable, they are normally good conversationalists (when you can get a word in), funny, witty, charming, and amusing.

On the negative side, the Proud Peacock tends to be so over the top and so self-centred, that they can get on your nerves, or make you feel uncomfortable or embarrassed if they are not careful. Why? Because sometimes they are so intense and self-centred, and their outrageousness is just too outrageous, inappropriate, or unwarranted for you, or the situation!

As Proud Peacocks live for drama, they tend to be very suggestible, and are the ones who are going to seek "help" for more "dramatic" problems. They are the ones who when they stub a toe, it's a broken leg, a headache is a brain tumour and a cough is Beriberi Disease (you get my drift!).

Because of this, Proud Peacocks tend to swing between feeling sky high and invincible, when life is great, and they are getting the attention and adulation they so want. On the flipside, they can easily get down, depressed and morose when they believe they are not centre-stage, or number one. This is where life is then seen as being awful, dreadful, and terrible. As you see, there is no middle ground with a Proud Peacock.

However, there can be another side to the Proud Peacock, a darker side that people find difficult to understand. Because they are often loud, extrovert, gregarious, and outgoing on a whole, the Proud Peacock often exudes the air in ultimate self-confidence, *but* often as not, this show of confidence is just a show – an act. Why? Because the Proud Peacocks needs that constant attention, alongside the external validation to confirm to them that they are actually OK. They constantly feed their inner confidence from other people and external factors all the while. The Proud Peacocks tend to be the ones with what I call "behind the painted smile syndrome". This is where they put a show onto the world about how wonderful their life is, and how super-duper confident they are, but in truth, they are hurting on some level, and don't want to show that vulnerability to their audience, and thus, put on this painted smile.

Interestingly, a lot of comedians, comics and comedy actors are prone to depression and troubled lives. The late Tony Hancock (*Hancock's Half Hour*) was Britain's favourite comedian in the 1950s and 1960s. In private he was a serial worrier and depressive who became an alcoholic. He committed suicide in Australia aged just 44. The late actor Robin Williams was one of many comedians who made people laugh, while simultaneously struggling with a personal darkness and depression, and later committed suicide in 2014. The comedy actress and writer, the late Caroline Ahern died in 2016 of cancer. But was plagued by depression and alcoholism throughout her career.

Peter Cook, John Cleese, Ruby Wax, Jack Dee, Stephen Fry, Spike Milligan, Robbie Williams and David Walliams are among the others who have spoken about their inner turmoil in the past.

Think of the Proud Peacock represented by the colour YELLOW. As yellow represents happiness, positivity, joy and laughter.  It can also represent cowardice, lack of moral fibre, one-upmanship and deceit.

# Typical traits of the Proud Peacock Personality Type

| | | |
|---|---|---|
| EASILY SHOWS HOW THEY ARE FEELING | LIKES TO BE CENTRE OF ATTENTION | EXTROVERTED |
| DEMONSTRATIVE | LIFE & SOUL OF THE PARTY/ STAR OF THE SHOW | LOUD |
| GOOD SENSE OF FUN | BUBBLY | AMUSING |
| CONFIDENT | 'BEHIND THE PAINTED SMILE' SYNDROME | EXCITABLE |
| OVER-REACTIVE | EMOTIONALLY- DRAMATIC | PASSIONATE |
| SUGGESTIBLE | ZEALOUS | FRIENDLY |
| GREGARIOUS | CREATIVE | EXAGGERATED FACIAL EXPRESSIONS |
| CATATROPHISES | LIKES TO SHOCK | UNCONVENTIONAL |
| SELF-CENTRED | SELFISH | SELF-ASSURED |
| OVERBEARING | OVER-EXCITABLE | SELF-CENTRED |

**Time to think, reflect and to record your findings here:**

**Exercise Five**

## How would you score yourself within the four personality types?

As we previously said, there are many different models to measure personality. But in the model, I have used here, we have looked at the four personality types of the White Dove, the Serene Swan, the Ruling Rooster, and the Proud Peacock.

Have a good read back on what you have identified, written, and reflected about the White Dove, the Serene Swan, the Ruling Rooster, and the Proud Peacock personality types. And how they relate to you, and what traits you recognise in yourself, on both a positive and negative level.

Listed below is a general synopsis of the four personality types:

| WHITE DOVE | SERENE SWAN | RULING ROOSTER | PROUD PEACOCK |
|---|---|---|---|
| Caring | Deep thinker | Wants to be in charge | Dramatic |
| Kind | Likes routine | Strong leader | Sociable |
| Sensitive | Desires control | Takes no prisoners | Good fun |
| Emotional | Obsessive | Focused | Self-Centred |
| Self-blaming | Selfish | Inattentive to detail | Suggestible |
| Instant gratification | Tenacious | Risk taker | Attention Seeking |

Now think about what percentage (%) of each personality type do you exhibit (e.g. 60% White Dove, 25% Proud Peacock. 5% Ruling Rooster and 10% Serene Swan). REMEMBER – we are a mixture of all 4, but with a predominate type, and the other three there as the support act!

| WHITE DOVE | SERENE SWAN | RULING ROOSTER | PROUD PEACOCK |
|---|---|---|---|
| % | % | % | % |

Total Score = 100 %

### Exercise Six

How would you score your partner, friends, family and loved ones within the four personality types?

| Name of Person | White Dove | Serene Swan | Ruling Rooster | Proud Peacock | Total |
|---|---|---|---|---|---|
| | % | % | % | % | 100% |
| | % | % | | % | 100% |
| | % | % | | % | 100% |
| | % | % | | % | 100% |

**Exercise Seven**

Just for fun. How would you personally score the 5 famous people below, within the four personality types?

| Name of Famous Person | Record your findings here | | | | |
| --- | --- | --- | --- | --- | --- |
| | White Dove | Serene Swan | Ruling Rooster | Proud Peacock | Total |
| Harry Kane<br><br>(Footballer) | % | % | % | % | 100% |
| Sheryl Sandberg<br><br>(COO Facebook) | % | % | % | % | 100% |
| Ed Sheeran<br><br>(Singer/Song writer) | % | % | % | % | 100% |
| Theresa May<br><br>(Prime Minister) | % | % | % | % | 100% |
| Sir David Attenborough<br><br>(TV/Nature) | % | % | % | % | 100% |
| Kate Middleton, Duchess of Cambridge<br><br>(Royal Family) | % | % | % | % | 100% |

**Time to think, reflect and to record your findings here:**

**Your plan of action:**

1. What have you learned from completing this chapter?

2. What are you going to do next to improve/better yourself?

3. Is what you want to achieve realistic, and within your scope or abilities/capabilities?

4. How would you know if you were successful in achieving it?

> **"Two things define your personality, the way you manage things when you have nothing, and the way you behave when you have everything".**
> **Unknown**

# The 6th C

## Is for
# Career Characteristics & Choices

### Qualities: Traits: Quirks

**Finding a career that fits your personality type, your personal values, strengths, weaknesses, and interests**

---

**"Your work is going to fill a large part of your life, and the only way to be truly satisfied is to do what you believe is great work. And the only way to do great work is to love what you do."**

**Steve Jobs**

---

### Aims

The aim of this chapter is for you to look more in-depth at personality type and traits, strengths, weaknesses, and interests.

### Objectives

The objective is for you to read the chapter and complete the given exercises to help you recognise what strengths, weaknesses, and interests are best suited to you and your job, career or business.

**Let us reflect on what you want to achieve from this chapter here:**

We have looked at the 4 personality types and personality traits in the previous chapter.

So, let us look more in-depth at what you enjoy doing, what you are good at, what interests you and what job you are best suited at, based on these parameters, whatever the industry, sector, or job title.

Listed below are 6 worker-type based personalities. Which coincide with the 4 personality types of the: White Dove, Serene Swan, Ruling Rooster and Proud Peacock. These 6 worker-type based personalities take it more in-depth by using a combination of the Holland Code model of career testing and psycho-analysis, to get you to look at your skills, strengths, weaknesses, likes and dislikes in the workplace, and the different career options, that go with that personality, skillset, and interests.

That is why my career and personality coaching can help you for the job, career, or business best suited to you, your personality and way of thinking, feeling, and behaving.

The 6 worker-type based personalities are:

The Practical Worker Type
The Analytical Worker Type
The Artistic Worker Type
The Helper Worker Type
The Influencer Worker Type
The Orderly Work Type Personality

## The Lark and Her Young Ones

A lark had made her nest in the early spring on the young green wheat. The brood had almost grown to their full strength and attained the use of their wings and the full plumage of their feathers, when the owner of the field, looking over his ripe crop, said, "The time has come when I must ask all my neighbours to help me with my harvest." One of the young Larks heard his speech and related it to his mother, inquiring of her to what place they should move for safety. "There is no occasion to move yet, my son," she replied; "the man who only sends to his friends to help him with his harvest is not really in earnest." The owner of the field came again a few days later and saw the wheat shedding the grain from excess of ripeness. He said, "I will come myself tomorrow with my laborers, and with as many reapers as I can hire, and will get in the harvest." The Lark on hearing these words said to her brood, "It is time now to be off, my little ones, for the man is in earnest this time; he no longer trusts his friends but will reap the field himself."

The moral of the story is self-help is the best help.

*From Aesop's Fables*

**Exercise One**

**Career Assessment: skillset, interests, and strengths**

This exercise will help you to determine your strongest skills, strengths, interests, and personality traits to help you look at different career, job, or business options. However, just because you may be good at something, or have done it in the past, it doesn't mean you want to do it anymore.

1. **Look at the following skills, strengths, and interests below**

2. **Highlight which ones you see or recognise in yourself**

3. **Measure them against the 6 work-based personality types**

| Adapting | Administrative | Advising | Analysing |
|---|---|---|---|
| Appraising | Assembling | Assessing | Auditing |
| Briefing | Budgeting | Building | Buying |
| Calculating | Capable | Calculating | Caring |
| Classifying | Certifying | Chairing | Changing |
| Charismatic | Charming | Coaching | Collating |
| Communicator | Computing | Conscientious | Constructing |
| Consulting | Controlling | Coordinating | Coping |
| Counselling | Creating | Creative | Cultivating |
| Decisive | Decisions | Delegating | Demonstrating |
| Designing | Detailing | Detecting | Determined |
| Developed | Developing | Diagnosing | Diplomacy |
| Directing | Displaying | Dissecting | Documenting |
| Doubtful | Drafting | Drawing | Driven |
| Driving | Editing | Educating | Empathising |
| Enforcing | Estimating | Evaluating | Examining |
| Excitable | Explaining | Explorer | Extrovert |
| Facilitator | Filing | Finalising | Finding |
| Finance | Financing | Fixing | Forecasting |
| Generator | Go-getter | Guide | Guiding |
| Handler | Helper | Helping | Helping-out |

| | | | |
|---|---|---|---|
| Implementing | Improving | Improvising | Influencing |
| Informing | Initiating | Innovative | Inspecting |
| Inspiring | Inspirational | Installing | Interpreting |
| Interviewing | Inventing | Investigating | Investigative |
| Judging | Juggles | Justifiable | Journalist |
| Labelling | Laborious | Language | Law |
| Leading | Learning | Lecturing | Legal |
| Lifting | Listening | Lifting | Listening |
| Making | Managing | Marketing | Measuring |
| Mediating | Memorising | Mentoring | Modelling |
| Moderating | Moderator | Motivating | Moving |
| Negotiating | Networking | Numeracy | Numbers |
| Obsessive | Observational | Organised | Organising |
| Operating | Operational | Ordered | Ordering |
| Painting | Persuading | Piloting | Pioneering |
| Planning | Precise | Precision | Presenting |
| Prioritising | Problems | Procuring | Proofreading |
| Promoting | Publicising | Publicist | Purchasing |
| Quality | Quantifying | Questioning | Quiet |
| Raising | Reconciling | Reconciliation | Recording |
| Recruiting | Rehabilitating | Relationships | Repairing |
| Repatriation | Reporting | Representing | Researching |
| Reserved | Responsible | Responsibility | Responsive |
| Restoring | Risk | Ruminates | Ruthless |
| Scheduler | Seller | Simplifier | Sorter |
| Story Teller | Structure | Summariser | Sums |
| Supervising | Supervision | Systems | Systematic |
| Teacher | Teaching | Team building | Testing |
| Tester | Trainer | Training | Tutoring |
| Unconventional | Understanding | Unlimited | Useful |
| Verbal | Versatile | Visualising | Volunteer |
| Waiting | Wanting | Worker | Writing |

| | |
|---|---|
| Time Management | Working to deadlines |
| Working under pressure | Risk assessment |
| Trouble shooting | Problem Solving |

**What skills, knowledge, interests, and prior experience do you recognise in yourself? Please record your findings here:**

# The Practical Worker Type

| Practical | Realistic | Analytical |
|-----------|-----------|------------|
| Careful | Organised | Researcher |
| Thorough | Watchful | Meticulous |

People who are the practical and realistic work type workers, are the ones who prefer an independent, hands-on type of approach to problems and solutions.

The practical worker type likes to work in the real world and enjoys using their eyes, hands, and bodies when working in a practical, useful, and functional way.

The practical worker type likes solving concrete instead of abstract problems. And solves problems by looking at the problem constructively, and then doing something physical in solving it.

The practical worker type prefers working with physical things, such as objects, materials, tools, machines, plants, and animals.

Many of the practical worker type occupations are often quite physical, manual type of work that requires working outside. And quite often does not involve a lot of paperwork or working closely with others.

The occupations the practical worker type is ideally suited to working with animals, tools, materials or machinery.

Here are some of the occupations that suit the Practical Worker
Type:

| Builder | Bricklayer | Plumber |
|---|---|---|
| Electrician | Roofer | Gardener |
| Carpenter | Assembler | Repairer |
| Cook/Chef | Sheet Metal Worker | Car Mechanic |
| Plant/Machine Operator | Aircraft Serviceman | Installer |
| Machinery Mechanic | Computer Programmer | Farmer |

**?** **What aspect of the Practical Worker Type do you recognise in yourself?**

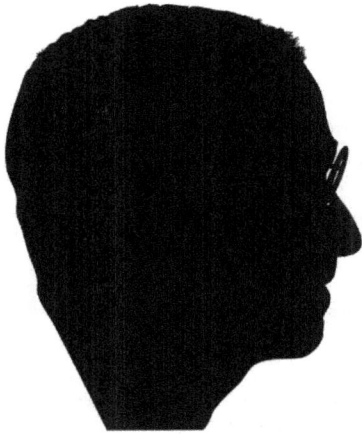

# The Analytical Worker Type

| Bright | Analytical | Problem-solving |
|---|---|---|
| Creating | Thinking | Designing |
| Organising | Resolving | Understanding |

People who are the analytical work type personality, are the ones who prefer the logical, investigative, analytical, intellectual, and scholarly types of problems and approaches. They are the one who like to research, collect, and analyse the information before making decisions, or taking any kind of action.

The analytical worker type are often unconventional and independent thinkers, who are curious and very insightful who enjoy using their minds and their intellect. But they are often quite introverted and lack leadership and persuasive skills.

The analytical worker type likes to read, study, use books and other data instead of working hands-on. If they are working outside in the field, it would be in a purely research or investigative base capacity only, and not because of the physical aspect of their work.

The analytical worker type prefers to deal with the real world from a distance, rather than associate with people and things that are considered close-up and personal.

The occupations the analytical worker type is ideally suited to involve working independently and focus on solving abstract, complex, investigative problems in original ways.

**Here are some of the occupations that suit the Analytical Worker Type:**

| | | |
|---|---|---|
| Investigative Journalist | Historian | Structural/Civil Engineer |
| IT Applications Programmer | Judge | Researcher |
| Archaeologist | Police Detective | Surgeon |
| Food Scientist | Electrical Engineer | University Professor |
| Actuary | Statistician | Diplomat |
| Strategist | Negotiator | Private Investigator |

**?** **What aspect of the Analytical Work Type Personality do you recognise in yourself?**

# The Artistic Worker Type

| Creative | Creating | Designing |
|---|---|---|
| Specialising | Researching | Expression |
| Visionary | Awareness | Artistic |

People who are the artistic worker type are impulsive, impetuous, independent, and creative, and requires the need for self-expression with lots of spirit, enthusiasm, and focus.

The artistic worker type uses their hands, body, mind, and imagination to create new things through the medium of sight, sound, and textures, and is especially sensitive to colour, form, sound and feeling.

The artistic worker type solves problems by creating something new, and creativity can also be expressed by an artistic personality type with data and systems. The artistic worker type often excels at working with forms, designs, and patterns.

The artistic worker type often requires self-expression and work that can be done without following a clear set of rules. They prefer to work alone and independently, in an unstructured, free-flowing situation that requires self-expression. Rather than working in rigid and structured teams or with others that determine the outcome or workload.

The occupations the artistic worker type is ideally suited to working creatively, by creating, designing, inspiring, and influencing for people to buy, watch, look at, wear, adorn, or to shock and take umbrage.

**Here are some of the occupations that suit the Artistic Worker Type:**

| Stage Performer | Artist | Musician |
|---|---|---|
| Writer | Photographer | Journalist |
| Interior Designer | Game Designer | Window Dresser |
| Floral Arranger | Goldsmith/Silversmith | Designer |
| Hair Stylist | Make-Up Artist | Film Director |
| Choreographer | Film/Documentary Maker | Landscape Gardener |

**?** **What aspect of the Artistic Work Type Personality do you recognise in yourself?**

## The Helper Worker Type

| Helping | Caring | Nurturing |
|---------|---------|-----------|
| Leading | Teaching | Mentoring |
| Guiding | Creating | Solving |

People who are the helper worker types are those who are kind, caring, friendly and sociable people. Who are sensitive to people's moods and feelings and can make friends easily.

The helper worker type main driver is to focus all their attention on people and their concerns and try and fix or help them. But sometimes they focus too much on people's concerns to the exclusion of anything else and they can become quite overbearing or obsessive.

The helper worker type operates through words, thoughts, and feelings, alongside empathy, intuition and gut reaction and sensitivity to emotional cues and body language. This is what helps them solve 'people problems', sometimes before others are even aware of them.

Because of this, the helper type is highly skilled at helping, advising, guiding, informing, training, developing, and curing people.

The occupations the helper work type personality is ideally suited to involve communicating with, and/or helping, teaching, or supporting people. These occupations often involve helping or providing a service to others.

**Here are some of the occupations that suit the Helper Worker Type:**

| Teacher | Carer | Advisor |
|---|---|---|
| Counsellor / Psychotherapist | Nanny | Social Worker |
| Doctor | Nurse | Dentist |
| Paramedic | Ambulance Driver | Vet |
| Mediator | Employment Recruiter | Speech Therapist |
| Flight Attendant | Physiotherapist | Check Out/Till Operator |

**?** **What aspect of the Helper Work Type Personality do you recognise in yourself?**

# The Influencer Worker Type

| Influential | Persuasive | Leader |
|:---:|:---:|:---:|
| Focused | Tenacious | Determined |
| Organised | Bold | Assertive |

People who are the influencer worker types are the ones who like to lead and take charge and be in total control of the situation and focus solely on a project in hand. This is achieved by working with people, to influence, persuade, manipulate, lead, and take charge.

Your influencer worker type is the one that wants to be the top of the tree, the top of their game or the best in their field. They enjoy the money, power, status, lifestyle and trapping that this brings them, and will not let anything get in their way.

The influencer worker type solves problems by taking calculated risks. They research and calculate the probabilities and do not rely on gut reaction or intuition about what will work or not.

The influencer worker types are often calm, confident and in control. They are assertive introverts who are enthusiastic decision-makers. Their decisions are not based on emotion and they do not notice the personal concerns of others or of themselves.

The occupations the influencer worker type is ideally suited to focus on taking charge, starting up and carrying out projects. These occupations can involve leading people, making many decisions, risk-taking. Influencers often deal with business or run their own businesses.

**Here are some of the occupations that suit the Influencer Worker Type:**

| | | |
|---|---|---|
| Editor-In-Chief | Gallery Owner | Advertising Agency Owner |
| Producer | Company Owner | Estate Agent |
| Finance Manager | Head Teacher | Logistics Manager |
| Lawyer / Solicitor | Sales Manager | Marketing Manager |
| Head Groundsman | HR Manager | Hotel Manager |
| Management Consultant | Barrister | Company Director |

**?** What aspect of the Influencer Work Type Personality do you recognise in yourself?

# The Orderly Work Type Personality

| Organising | Detailed | Factual |
|---|---|---|
| Analytical | Accuracy | Reliability |
| Creating | Designing | Solving |

People who are the orderly worker type like to work in a factual and orderly fashion, with numbers, data, facts, and figures. They like to carry out these tasks in minute detail by using their mind, eyes, and hands.

The orderly worker type is quiet, careful, neat, orderly, practical methodical, responsible, well-organised and task oriented. They are the ones that like to follow the rules and prefer to carry out tasks initiated by others, rather than being in a position of authority.

The orderly worker type solves problems by using their logical and ordered mind to fact-find and put things into order.

The orderly worker type has a strong need to feel safe, secure, and certain. They achieve this by following a routine to get things finished by taking care of every detail.

The occupations the orderly work type personality is ideally suited involve following set procedures and routines and working with data and details more than with ideas. They often excel at administration and clerical-based occupations, where there is usually a clear line of authority to follow. They can easily work by themselves through their own initiative or in part of a team.

**Here are some of the occupations that suit the Orderly Worker Type:**

| Proof Reader | Translator | Copy Editor |
|---|---|---|
| Police Inspector | Tax Inspector | Filing Clerk |
| Finance Clerk | Database Designer | Accountant |
| Payroll Clerk | Quality Control Inspector | Legal Secretary |
| IT Systems Administrator | Postal Sorter | Distribution Clerk |
| Bank Clerk | Mortgage Clerk | Medical Secretary |
| Computer Programmer | Notary | Web Developer |

**?** **What aspect of the Orderly Work Type Personality do you recognise in yourself?**

## The Little Red Hen

There once was a farm with a big red barn. And in that big red barn, there lived many animals, the smallest of which, was a little red hen.

The little red hen may have been little, but she was the most active resident of the farm. When she wasn't laying eggs, she spent her time clucking and walking about the barn, pecking at the seeds on the ground, or gathering up twigs and hay to make her nest. She kept everything in the barn tidy and clean.

One day, while she was pecking at the ground, she discovered some leftover wheat grains that the farmer had left behind. She knew that the wheat could be planted, and then made into delicious fresh bread.

So, she went to the pigsty, where the pig was eating from a bucket of slop.

"Uh, Excuse me, cluck, cluck, I need someone to help me plant this wheat," said the little red hen.

"Oink Oink, Not I," said the pig, as he went back to his slop.

So, the little red hen went outside, and found the cat, lying in the sun and playing with a ball of yarn.

"Uh Cluck Cluck, will you help me plant this wheat?" said the little red hen.

"Meow," said the cat. "Not I. Can't you see that I'm busy? Meow."

The little red hen was frustrated, but she did not give up. She walked all the way out to the pond, where the duck was lazing around in the cool water.

"Cluck cluck, will you help me plant this wheat?" said the little red hen.

"Quack, quack, Not I. Maybe I will help you later, when I am finished with my swim," said the duck.

"Cluck cluck, then I will do it myself," said the little red hen.

So, the little red hen went off on her own, out to the field, and found a nice spot to plant the wheat. When she was finished, she went back to the barn to rest.

Soon, when the wheat had grown tall and golden yellow, the hen became excited to make bread from it. But first, she had to harvest it.

"Cluck, who will help me cut the wheat?" asked the little red hen.

"Not I," oinked the pig, who was lying in some mud.

"Not I," meowed the cat, who was taking a catnap.

"Not I," quacked the duck, as he waddled back to the pond.

"Cluck Cluck, then I will do it myself," said the little red hen.

Once the wheat had been ground into flour, the little red hen knew it was time to bake the bread.

"Cluck, who will help me bake the bread?" she asked, although she already predicted what the answer would be.

"Not I," oinked the pig.

"Not I," meowed the cat.

"Not I," quacked the duck.
"Cluck cluck, then I will do it myself," said the little red hen.

So, she made the flour into a loaf of bread, and put it into the oven. Then, she sat and rested. Soon, as the bread become hot and soft, the air filled with the sweet smell of freshly baked bread. The pig and the cat and the duck all came running into the big red barn.

"Uh, who will help me eat this bread?

Cluck! Who will help me eat this bread?" said the little red hen.

"I will!" oinked the pig.

"I will!" meowed the cat.

"I will!" quacked the duck.

"Cluck cluck, well," said the hen,

"Did you help me plant the wheat, and did you help me harvest the wheat, and did you help me mill the wheat, and did you help me bake the bread?"

The other animals all shook their heads no.

"Then I will eat the bread myself," said the little red hen. And, she did.

An old Russian folklore tale that teaches the virtues of work ethic and personal initiative

**Your plan of action:**

1. What have you learned from completing this chapter?

2. What are you going to do next to improve/better yourself?

3. Is what you want to achieve realistic, and within your scope or abilities/capabilities?

4. How would you know if you were successful in achieving it?

> "Challenge yourself, grow, blossom, and become who you were meant to be. Don't ever stay at a job solely out of convenience or comfort. Aim higher, even if that means pursuing another job that's just one step closer to your ultimate goal."
>
> Carolyn Aronson

## Inspiration Time

Please find below, an inspiration piece, that was written by Paul Simmonds This piece reflects his hard work, determination, motivation, and positive thinking, that has gotten him to where he is today. A self-made millionaire and serial entrepreneur.

## From Past to Present

From an early age I'd dreamt of being an entrepreneur and running my own successful business, but never actually thought it would become a reality. Leaving school without even taking any exams, I joined the army at 15 years old. This proved to be the making of me. I had not really applied myself up until the age of 16 and I soon realised that military life was going to be a steep learning curve.

Instead of cutting corners like I had in the past, I was determined to learn a trade and gain a qualification whole in the army. I took advantage of the courses available and the training sessions that I was able to do as part of my learning path. After completing a year at an apprentice college back in 1987, I moved on to the army trade training school in Catterick where I completed my trade training as a telecom engineer within the Royal Corps of Signals.

I was to spend a further 10 years in the army and I travelled the world, learning a lot of trade and life skills along the way. Prior to joining up, I didn't realise that the military had so many options available to gain work experience. I quite naively thought everyone in the army carried a gun. The options available really are unlimited, you can train to be anything from a doctor to a chef or a pilot to a policeman and the training I received was second to none.

After time in the army I decided to pursue a career in civvie street. I wanted to continue in the telecom arena, so I applied for a job in London as Head of Communications at the BMA (British Medical Association). I was keen to learn more than just the military side of communications and found the BMA offered more learning opportunities as well as management courses which I was keen to do as the thought of running my own business was definitely still in my head.

After 18 months at the BMA I decided to work as a telecom consultant offering my services to companies who required specific programming on their phone systems. I worked for a lot of call centres who had high volume customer calls and needed to multi-task using their computers and telephones.

I also completed a lot of training courses in the evenings. These specifically concentrated on individuals who were entrepreneurial and wanting to get to running their own business, they included learning about VAT rates, flow charts, PowerPoint presentations and accounting processes.

After working as a consultant, I took the leap of faith and set up my own telecoms company which consisted of me and an ex-RAF servicewoman who had skills in the admin and payroll arena, which would prove useful as I built the company up over the years.

Following several years of being successful with my first company, I joined forces with another entrepreneur and we then combined our companies to make a group of companies called Comms Group, we added to our portfolio by opening an IT department & web design department within the group which brought our internal staff total to 35 people.

Over a period of 8 years we continued to grow the business up until 2016 when the workload was so much that we joined forces with a PLC in London. The PLC bought out shares in Comms Group and added the group to their ever-expanding network of companies that they had acquired with many acquisitions over a period of 25 years.

At present I am the Managing Director at Comms Group and I report in to the CEO at AdEPT telecom – a company with an annual turnover of £50 million. On a daily basis, I still do the same as I did 30 years ago, but it's just on a much larger scale. I look back and think about the early days and joining the army, which actually defined the person I am today, with determination and self-belief we can achieve anything in life, it's just about applying ourselves to a specific task and seeing a job through.

I'm in a position where I could retire now aged 46, but I feel that there's still a lot to learn and working for a PLC has opened a lot of new doors with more opportunities, so while work is still exciting I will continue to literally live and learn.

### *Paul Simmons – Serial Entrepreneur*

I thought I would put in one of my favourite stories. If this doesn't inspire you, then I am struggling to think what will.

## The elephant and the rope

"There is a story about a man who, as he was passing some elephants, suddenly stopped, confused by the fact that these huge creatures were being held by only a small rope tied to their front leg. No chains, no cages. It was obvious that the elephants could, at any time, break away from their bonds but for some reason, they did not.
He saw a trainer nearby and asked why these animals just stood there and made no attempt to get away. "Well," the trainer said, "when they are very young and much smaller we use the same size rope to tie them and, at that age, it's enough to hold them. As they grow up, they are conditioned to believe they cannot break away. They believe the rope can still hold them, so they never try to break free."

The man was amazed. These animals could at any time break free from their bonds but because they believed they couldn't, they were stuck right where they were.

Like the elephants, how many of us go through life hanging onto a belief that we cannot do something, simply because we failed at it once before? I think every one of us can relate to this story and the feeling of having failed at something or another over the years. Over time, we can begin to think that we are not capable of doing a particular thing and we accept this as the truth and limit ourselves to a very confined world. We think to ourselves 'oh I tried that before and it didn't work out, what is the point in trying it again and wasting my time, I don't want to look like a fool!' And this is how we start to shrink and contract and settle for a life that is 'safe' and 'less than exciting'. However, if we could look at all the so-called 'failures' in our lives as just stepping stones along our path and decide to respond in a way that is positive, saying, 'oh well, at least I tried, now I know what doesn't work so it makes my next attempt clearer!' Treat it like a process of elimination, gathering momentum and staying focused on what we would like to achieve, trying this way and that until we succeed!

So, don't limit yourself to a small world, stop confining yourself to a life that is restricted, break free of your mental boundaries, and expand out into this magnificent place that we live in! The world is your oyster! Don't confine yourself any longer to the belief that you can't do something, shatter those thoughts and beliefs, and spread your wings and fly! YOU can do anything you set your heart on, if you just believe it! Go on, just try it, and never mind what the outcome is, just enjoy every experience you encounter in your life and embrace every bit of it! So, what if it takes you

10 attempts or 100! Which will you regret more…the things you did or the things you didn't do?! It's all a journey so let's make it AWESOME! You will never know how far you can go until you have the courage to do it! And if you fall, just get up again… that's all!

Just remember Winners Never Quit!


Paul Simmons

# The 7th C
## Is for
# Capabilities

**Capable: Able: Achievable**

# What skills and knowledge do you possess?

Identifying what you know, what you don't know you know, or what you had forgotten you know, or what you don't know you know yet

> **"An investment in knowledge pays the best interest".**
>
> **Benjamin Franklin**

## Aims

The aim of this chapter is for you to have more of an understanding of the different types of skills, knowledge, and attributes.

## Objectives

The objective is for you to read the chapter and complete the given exercises to help you grow, develop, and utilise your current skills. How? By understanding more about what skills, knowledge, competencies, and personal and physical attributes you have. And the impact it will have on you, and on your career or business.

**Let us reflect on what you want to achieve from this chapter here:**

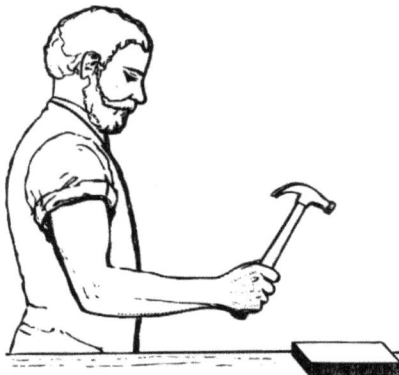

# Skills

**Skill**: from Old Norse *Skil* – meaning discernment, knowledge
and from late Old English *Scele* – meaning knowledge.

Skills are physical, practical, and emotional actions that you learn, which help you to do certain tasks. You might learn new skills through work, study, sport, or activities you do in your spare time.

Your skills are important because they help you show an employer why you should get a job.

If you're able to recognise and talk about your own skills, then you will find it easier to do things and recognise what areas are in which you can grow and develop to make those skills even better and stronger.

Skills can often be divided into two groups:

1. **General skills**
2. **Specific skills**

In the domain of work-based skills, general skills would include things like, teamwork, leadership, and time management.

In the domain of specific work-based skills, specific skills would include things like, typing, computer programming, laying a floor or driving a lorry.

Skills usually require a certain environmental stimuli and situations to assess the level of skill being shown and used.

## The Thief and the Innkeeper

A thief hired a room in a tavern and stayed a while in the hope of stealing something which should enable him to pay his reckoning. When he had waited some days in vain, he saw the Innkeeper dressed in a new and handsome coat and sitting before his door. The Thief sat down beside him and talked with him. As the conversation began to flag, the Thief yawned terribly and at the same time howled like a wolf. The Innkeeper said, "Why do you howl so fearfully?' "I will tell you," said the Thief, "but first let me ask you to hold my clothes, or I shall tear them to pieces. I know not, sir, when I got this habit of yawning, nor whether these attacks of howling were inflicted on me as a judgment for my crimes, or for any other cause; but this I do know, that when I yawn for the third time, I actually turn into a wolf and attack men." With this speech he commenced a second fit of yawning and again howled like a wolf, as he had at first. The Innkeeper. hearing his tale and believing what he said, became greatly alarmed and, rising from his seat, attempted to run away. The Thief laid hold of his coat and entreated him to stop, saying, "Pray wait, sir, and hold my clothes, or I shall tear them to pieces in my fury, when I turn into a wolf." At the same moment he yawned the third time and set up a terrible howl. The Innkeeper, frightened lest he should be attacked, left his new coat in the Thief's hand, and ran as fast as he could into the inn for safety. The Thief made off with the coat and did not return again to the inn.

The moral of the story is every tale is not to be believed.

*From Aesop's Fables*

# Knowledge

**Knowledge** – noun – meaning: Facts, information, and skills acquired through experience or education; the theoretical or practical understanding of a subject.

Whatever path you take, your previous skills, knowledge and experiences will be the currency you need to take you on your journey. And it is with these skills, knowledge, and experiences you will be able to barter for a more meaningful job, role, better job prospects, earn and make more money and live the life you want to live.

This chapter will help you understand and recognise all the key strengths, skills, and knowledge you possess. And what you need to work on or develop further, to get you to where you want to go.

Listed below are various skills sets:

- **Hard Skills**

- **Soft Skills**

- **Transferable Skills**

- **Competences & Competencies**

- **Personal and Physical Attributes**

- **Emotional Intelligence (EI)**

**Something for you to read and reflect on**

**This is a genuine job advert obtained from:**
https://www.healthcareers.nhs.uk/explore-roles/doctors/roles-doctors/surgery/neurosurgery/entry-requirements-skills-and-interests on 23.02.2018

These are the skills and interest needed for someone who wants to apply for a job as a Brain Surgeon in a UK NHS hospital.

## Entry requirements, skills, and interests (neurosurgery)

This page provides useful information about the entry requirements needed for this specialty up to and including foundation training. It also includes information on the skills and interests you will need.

## Entry requirements

Before you train as a surgeon you must complete a degree in medicine and have obtained a MBBS or equivalent qualification.

Find out more information about getting into medical school.

You then need to complete a two-year foundation programme. After successfully completing your first year of foundation training you become eligible for registration as a doctor with the General Medical Council (GMC). Foundation training includes undertaking rotations in a range of specialties including surgery.

To find information about the Foundation Programme, visit our page https://www.healthcareers.nhs.uk/i-am/working-health/information-doctors/foundation-training-programme/applying-foundation

After completing your foundation training, you need to undertake specialty training as in the training and development page.

Neurosurgery is a technically demanding surgical specialty.

You'll need a special blend of skills and personal qualities which include:

- A high degree of manual dexterity
- Good hand-eye co-ordination, excellent vision, and visuo-spatial awareness
- A blend of confidence and caution
- Good organisational ability and excellent communication skills
- Physical stamina to cope with long hours and demanding nature of the work
- Emotional strength to manage very sick patients
- The ability to lead and manage a team effectively
- Able to embrace change and constantly developing technologies
- A strong interest in anatomy and physiology

If you're applying for a role either directly in the NHS or in an organisation that provides NHS Services you'll be asked to show how you think the NHS values apply in your everyday work. The same will be true if you're applying for a university course funded by the NHS.

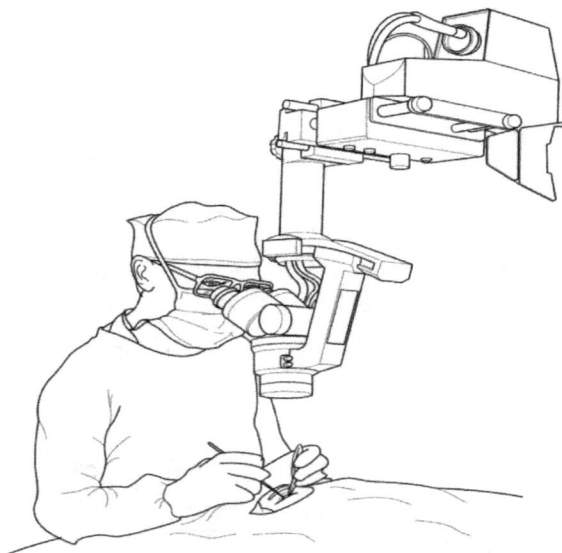

## Hard Skills

Hard skills are part of the skill-set that is required for a job or business. They include the expertise necessary for an individual to successfully do the job in hand. These types of skills are learned and can be defined, evaluated, and measured and benchmarked quite easily. Hard skills are those skills you can either do or not!

Hard skills are typically acquired through formal education and training programs, including college, university, apprenticeships, short-term training classes, online courses, certification programs, as well as through formal and informal on-the-job training.

Hard skills are the most commonly referred to during the hiring and interview process, to compare candidates for employment. They are job-specific and are typically listed in job postings and job descriptions.

In some industries, employers may even test candidates' hard skills, to make sure that they can really do what their CV's claims they can do. Once you have the job, your employer may evaluate your hard skills again, to see if you are suitable for a promotion or a transfer.

The 3 attributes for hard skills:

1. Hard skills are learning based skills

2. Hard skills take Smarts, Intelligence, or IQ (also known as your left brain-the logical centre)

3. Hard skills are skills where the rules or application stay the same, regardless of which company, circumstance, or people you work with

# Hard skills include:

- Reading
- Writing
- Mathematics
- Typing
- Shorthand
- Audio typing
- Taking minutes
- Proofreading/Editing
- Graphic Design
- Computer programming
- Programming (other)
- Accounting
- Bookkeeping
- Proficiency in a foreign language
- Familiarity with technical language (e.g. medical or legal)
- Law or Legal
- HR
- Translation
- Machine operation
- First-aid skills
- Health & Safety
- Risk Assessment
- Using word processing software (e.g. Word)
- Using spreadsheets (e.g. Excel)
- Using database software (e.g. Access)
- Using presentation software (e.g. PowerPoint)
- Use of telecommunications systems
- Data analysis skills
- The ability to operate certain machinery (e.g. fork lifts)
- Driving – including the ability to drive anything other than a car
- Practical Skills: Gas Engineer, Plumber, Electrician, Bricklayer, Plasterer, Glazier, Carpenter, Tiler, Gardener
- Playing a musical instrument

**Exercise One**

## Hard Skills recognition

In this exercise I want you to think about your TOP 10 hard skills that you possess. Think about where these 10 skills came from originally. And think about how you have expanded on them over time and record your findings below.

| | Your Hard Skill | Your findings |
|---|---|---|
| 1 | | |
| 2 | | |
| 3 | | |
| 4 | | |
| 5 | | |
| 6 | | |
| 7 | | |
| 8 | | |
| 9 | | |
| 10 | | |

# What have you learned from doing this exercise?

## Soft Skills

Soft skills are as important as hard skills in you getting your ideal job or having a successful business. But, what exactly are soft skills and why are they so important? Soft skills are those skills that have no formal training or qualifications and are open to interpretation. Soft skills can't be taught in a classroom or measured on paper as a qualification, they are learned from others around us, our environment, our life experiences, and societal skills and social pressures.

So, soft skills are interpersonal skills and are all about how you relate to yourself and to others around you. They include knowing how to get along with people; how to communicate articulately and effectively; being able to face and bounce back from adversity and setbacks; knowing how to problem solve effectively; displaying a positive mental attitude and growth mindset. All these qualities and skills are crucial for success.

The problem is, the importance of these soft skills is often undervalued or played down. Plus, there is far less training provided for them than hard skills and they are often quite difficult to define.

The 3 attributes of Soft Skills:

1. Most soft skills are not taught well in school, and are learned on the job or through life experiences by trial and error

2. Soft skills usually take Emotional Intelligence or EQ (also known as your right brain - the emotional centre)

3. Soft skills are skills where the rules change depending on your own perspective on the situation in hand, the company culture and ethos, and people that you work with.

## Soft skills include:

- Self-awareness
- Emotion regulation
- Resilience
- The ability to forgive and forget
- Persistence and perseverance
- Patience
- Perceptiveness
- Communication skills
- Teamwork skills
- Interpersonal relationship skills
- Presentation skills
- Meeting management skills
- Facilitating skills
- Selling skills
- Management skills
- Leadership skills
- Mentoring/coaching skills
- Managing skills
- Self-promotion skills
- Skills in dealing with difficult personalities
- Skills in dealing with difficult/unexpected situations
- Savvy in handling office politics
- Influence/persuasion skills
- Negotiation skills
- Networking skills
- Creativity
- Time-management
- Working on own initiative
- Strong work ethic
- Decisive
- Flexible
- Personal responsibility
- Empathy
- Respect
- Diplomacy
- Willingness
- Intuitive insight
- Approachability

**Exercise Two**

## Soft Skills recognition

In this exercise I want you to think about your TOP 10 soft skills that you possess. Think about where these 10 skills came from originally. And think about how you have expanded on them over time and record your findings below.

|  | Your Soft Skill | Your findings |
|---|---|---|
| 1 | | |
| 2 | | |
| 3 | | |
| 4 | | |
| 5 | | |
| 6 | | |
| 7 | | |
| 8 | | |
| 9 | | |
| 10 | | |

# What have you learned from doing this exercise?

## Transferable Skills

Transferable skills are a core set of skills, knowledge, abilities, and experiences, which can be applied to a wide range of different jobs and industries. They are those skills which you have been using in one job, industry, sector, or business to get the job done. They are usually picked up over time, and can be gained from previous positions, charity, or voluntary work, from outside hobbies, interests, or passions or even from experience at home.

So, why are transferable skills so important? Although transferable skills are slightly "softer" than hard skills, or those skills that are directly related to a position. Transferable skills are incredibly valuable to employers, as they show an attitude to learning and how much a person has learnt from previous positions or experiences. They can also bring another perspective or dynamic to the job role. But the great thing about transferable skills is they are a great way to showcase that you can be a great fit for the role, regardless of what position you are going for or what business you want to set up. And the best part? Everyone has them.

If you're currently lacking experience in the field you're looking for work in, transferable skills can be a great way to highlight why you're right for the role and what you can bring. Examples of when this can be helpful include graduates, entry-level positions, redundancy, returning to work after some time out (after having a baby, ill health, sabbatical or travel etc), changing careers, or setting up your own business.

# The 3 attributes of transferable skills

1. Most transferable skills are a mixture of academic, learning on the job and through life experiences by trial and error.

2. Transferable skills are a combination of Smarts, Intelligence, or IQ (also known as your left brain-the logical centre) and Emotional Intelligence or EQ (also known as your right brain-the emotional centre).

3. Transferable skills are skills where the rules can either change depending on your own perspective on the situation in hand, or they are absolute, where the rules or application stay the same. These are both dependent on the job in hand, the company's policies and procedures, the people you are working with and how they want things done

---

"Regardless of profession or title, at some level we are all hired to do the same job. We are all problem solvers, paid to anticipate, identify, prevent, and solve problems within our areas of expertise. This applies to any job, at any level, in any organization, anywhere in the world, and being aware of this is absolutely vital to job search and career success in any field."

Martin Yate, Knock 'Em Dead 2016: The Ultimate Job Search Guide

---

# Transferable skills include the ability to:

- Listening skills to understand oral instructions
- Good listener/listening skills
- Approachability
- Give verbal instructions
- Learn new procedures
- Understand and carry out written instructions
- Orally convey information to others
- Observe and assess others' performances
- Written communication skills
- Mathematical processes to solve problems
- Speak/talk in public
- Demonstrate professionalism
- Work in a professional environment
- Provide constructive criticism
- Give feedback
- Negotiate, persuade, and influence people
- Motivate others
- Handle complaints
- Train or teach new skills
- Delegate work to others
- Oversee others' work
- Counsel people
- Build strong customer relationships
- Collaborate with other people
- Mentor younger colleagues
- Mentor new starters/new staff
- Resolve conflicts
- Develop relationships with suppliers
- Demonstrate comfort when dealing with all people
- Gain clients' or customers' confidence
- Oversee budgets
- Recruit personnel
- Review resumes
- Interview perspective job candidates
- Select new hires
- Supervise employees
- Allocate resources such as equipment, materials, and facilities
- Schedule personnel

- Presiding over meetings
- Negotiating contracts
- Evaluate personnel
- Organize committees
- Perform general clerical and administrative support tasks
- Design forms, correspondence, and reports
- Manage records
- Take minutes at meetings
- Type up the minutes from the meetings
- Use word processing software
- Use database management software
- Use spreadsheet software
- Use desktop publishing software
- Use presentation software
- Perform data entry
- Keep track of accounts receivable, accounts payable, billing, etc. (bookkeeping)
- Budgeting
- Buying
- Answer the phone
- Screen telephone calls
- Meet and greet visitors
- Identify and present problems to upper management
- Anticipate and prevent problems from occurring or reoccurring
- Use critical thinking skills to make decisions or evaluate possible solutions to problems
- Problem solve or solve problems
- Deal with obstacles and crises
- Define organization's or department's needs
- Set goals
- Prioritise tasks
- Locate and reach out to suppliers or sub-contractors
- Analyse information and forecast results
- Manage your time effectively
- Meet deadlines
- Plan and implement events and activities
- Develop and implement new policies and procedures
- Develop a budget
- Coordinate and develop programs
- Document procedures and results
- Produce reports

- Conduct research using the Internet and library resources
- Generate ideas
- Develop and carry out ideas
- Use computer software that is related to job
- Use job-related equipment
- Install software on computers
- Use the Internet
- Use e-mail and search engines
- Use equipment such as printers, copiers, and fax machines
- Troubleshoot problems with hardware, software, and other equipment
- Install equipment
- Troubleshoot problems with and repair equipment
- Maintain equipment
- Inspect equipment to identify problems
- Demonstrate fluency or working knowledge of a foreign language
- Demonstrate fluency or working knowledge of sign language
- Fundraise
- Write grants
- Design websites
- Cooking
- Gardening
- Cleaning
- Flower Arranging
- Looking after a pet or animal
- Looking after a sick, infirm, or disabled relative, spouse or friend
- Nursing

**Exercise Three**

**Transferable Skills recognition**

In this exercise I want you to think about your TOP 10 transferable skills that you possess. Think about where these 10 skills came from originally. And think about how you have expanded on them over time and record your findings below.

| | Your Transferable Skill | Your findings |
|---|---|---|
| 1 | | |
| 2 | | |
| 3 | | |
| 4 | | |
| 5 | | |
| 6 | | |
| 7 | | |
| 8 | | |
| 9 | | |
| 10 | | |

# What have you learned from doing this exercise?

# Competence vs Competencies

**Competence** – noun:
The ability to do something well or efficiently
A range of skills or abilities
A specific ability or skill

The best (and simplest) definition I found is: Though both having similar meanings, **Competence** and **Competencies** are used in different contexts.

**Competence** refers to **WHAT** skills, knowledge, or abilities a person possesses.

So, competence is a cluster of related skills, knowledge, understanding, experience, and abilities, that demonstrate the person can act effectively, skilfully, proficiently, or mastery to the job or situation in hand.

**Competencies** refers to **HOW** a person describes how they use and incorporate those skills, knowledge, or abilities, and at what level.

So, competencies specify the 'how' (as opposed to the 'what') of performing job tasks, or what the person needs to do the job successfully.

Competencies, therefore incorporate the skills. But are **MORE** than the skill itself. They include the attitudes, abilities, and behaviours, as well as knowledge and understanding that is fundamental to the use of a skill.

Competencies are often used to help interviewers/recruiters/managers identify how a person would go about demonstrating one particular area of their skills, knowledge, and understanding in a certain situation. By describing **HOW** they would do it. And give examples of prior knowledge and experience of how they have achieved it. This is known as a competency-based questioning.

## The STAR Technique

Competency-based questions make up a large part of most job interviews. And from a company's point of view, they allow an objective assessment of a candidate's experience, and the qualities that make them suitable for the job. By using a series of structured questions that require people to answer these types of questions. It is easier for the employer to compare all the people who are applying for the job and their answers in a methodical and structured way.

Thankfully, there's a tried and tested technique that will help you to answer these tricky situations called **The STAR Technique**.

The STAR Technique is based on four structured answers that are all interlinked to each other from the previous answer.

---

**The STAR Technique**

**S = SITUATION**
WHAT is happening?

**T = TASK**
WHAT do I need to do to resolve it?

**A = ACTION**
HOW did I resolve it?

**R = RESULT**
WHAT was the result/outcome?

---

By using this step-by-step method, you will be able to answer each question in a systematic manner, without forgetting the important stuff.

Let us look at the 4 stages of The STAR Technique interview method in more detail.

**Which questions need a STAR response?**

Most STAR questions will usually start like asking you to:

**"Tell me about a time when you . . ."** followed by one of those competencies that have been listed on the job specification.

It is important to be familiar with these competencies, so that you can be prepared to give your answer, based on own personal experiences.

A lot of the questions will require you to think about past work experiences you've had. For those who are applying for Internships, Apprenticeships or have no previous work experience, you can still talk about any projects, extra-curricular activities, sports, hobbies, or interests. Or what you achieved while being at school, college, or university that bears relevance to the questions in hand.

On average, each of these four questions take 2 – 4 minutes to answer.

# The STAR Technique in more depth:

## 1. Situation

This is about setting the scene, giving a context and background to the situation.

## 2. Task

This is more specific to your exact role in the situation. You need to make sure that the interviewer knows what you were tasked with, rather than the rest of the team.

## 3. Action

This is the most important part of the STAR technique, because it allows you to highlight what action you took, and what your response was.

Remember, you need to talk about what you *specifically* did, so using the 'I' or 'Me', rather than 'Us' or 'We'. Otherwise you won't be showing off the necessary skills the employer is looking for.

Be sure to share a lot of detail, the interviewer will not be familiar with your history, although remember to avoid any acronyms, slang, or institutional language.

What you're trying to get across here is how you assessed and decided what was the appropriate response to the situation, and how you got the other team members involved – which in turn is a great way to demonstrate your communication skills.

## 4. Result

Ideally the result should be a positive one. The interviewer will also want to know what you learnt from that situation, and if there was anything you would do differently the next time if you were faced with the same or similar situation.

**Exercise Four**

## Your own personal STAR Technique question

Using the 4 step STAR questioning Technique, please answer the following question:

**"Tell me about your greatest career accomplishment to date...."**

| | |
|---|---|
| **SITUATION** | |
| **TASK** | |
| **ACTION** | |
| **RESULT** | |

**Time to think, reflect and to record your findings here:**

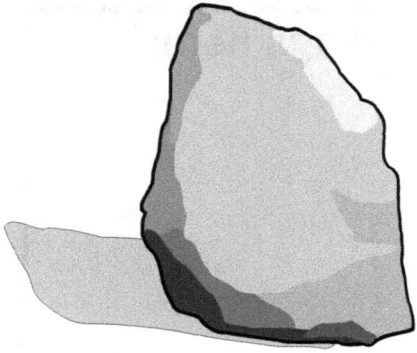

## The obstacle in our path

In ancient times, a King had a boulder placed on a roadway. He then hid himself and watched to see if anyone would move the boulder out of the way. Some of the king's wealthiest merchants and courtiers came by and simply walked around it.

Many people loudly blamed the King for not keeping the roads clear, but none of them did anything about getting the stone out of the way.

A peasant then came along carrying a load of vegetables. Upon approaching the boulder, the peasant laid down his burden and tried to push the stone out of the road. After much pushing and straining, he finally succeeded.

After the peasant went back to pick up his vegetables, he noticed a purse lying in the road where the boulder had been. The purse contained many gold coins and a note from the King explaining that the gold was for the person who removed the boulder from the roadway.

**Origin of story unknown**
The moral of the story is every obstacle we come across in life gives us an opportunity to improve our circumstances.

# Personal and Physical Attributes

**Attribute/s** – noun – meaning a quality or feature regarded as a characteristic or inherent part of someone or something.

Personal and physical attributes are those personal qualities, quirks and features that help to define you and your personality. Employers are interested to know more about who you are as a person, and what personal and physical attributes you have. These attributes are often just as important to employer as hard skills are. Why? Because it is these personal and physical attributes and characteristics that will determine if you are going to be a 'good fit' in a company or business, and fit in and adhere to, and with their ethos, values, and company standards.

**Here are some personal attributes**

| Sincere | Honest | Understanding |
|---------|--------|---------------|
| Kind | Caring | Loyal |
| Trustworthy | Dependable | Open-minded |
| Wise | Considerate | Good-natured |
| Friendly | Open | Warm |
| Good fun | Reliable | Courteous |
| Unselfish | Warm-hearted | Likeable |

**Here are some physical attributes**

| Blonde | Brunette | Red Haired |
|--------|----------|------------|
| Silver/Grey Haired | Tall | Short |
| Rosy | Pale-skinned | Dark-skinned |
| Slim | Fat | Thin |
| Blue-Eyed | Brown-Eyed | Green-Eyed |
| Green-Eyed | Grey-Eyed | Pierced |
| Tattooed | Smelly | Scarred |
| Clean | Dirty | Scruffy |

**Exercise Five**

## Personal and Physical Attributes match

This exercise is to get you to have a look at what personal and physical attributes you can match yourself to, in certain job roles.

This exercise is purely subjective as we all see ourselves from our own perspective and viewpoint.

| Job Role | Personal Attributes | Physical Attributes |
|---|---|---|
| Air Host/Hostess | | |
| Nurse | | |
| Solicitor | | |
| Tattoo Artist | | |
| Managing Director | | |

**Exercise Six**

## Personal and Physical Attributes match to your perfect job

Thinking about your perfect job, career, or business, what personal and physical attributes can you bring?

| My perfect job, career or business is: |
| --- |
|  |

| Personal Attributes | Physical Attributes |
| --- | --- |
|  |  |

**Time to think, reflect and to record your findings here:**

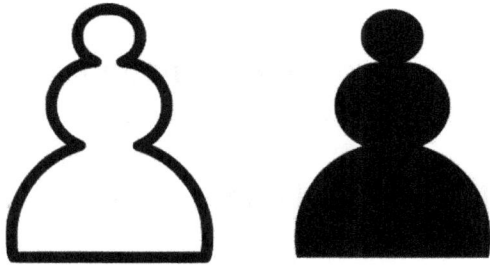

## Emotional Intelligence (EI)

I should imagine that most of you have never heard of Emotional Intelligence, yet alone even know what it is. And how important it is in attaining success in your career, and the way you want to live your life.

So, what is Emotional Intelligence (EI) - and why is it so important? Emotional Intelligence (EI) or Emotional Quotient (EQ) is a term created by two researchers – Peter Salavoy and John Mayer – and was popularised by Dan Goleman in his 1996 book of the same name.

**EI is defined as the ability to:**

- Recognise, understand, and manage our own emotions

- Recognise, understand, and influence the emotions of others

So, Emotional Intelligence (EI) is the ability to identify and manage your own emotions and the emotions of others. In today's fast-paced world, our success is highly dependent on our ability to read other people's signals and react appropriately to them. Therefore, every one of us, must develop the maturity to grow and develop our emotional intelligence skills required, to communicate more effectively with others.

Today we are going to have a look at the five major categories of emotional intelligence skills, that are recognised by researchers in this area. This is used extensively in career, business, and leadership.

**Understanding the Five Categories of Emotional Intelligence (EQ)**

**1. Self-awareness.** The ability to recognise an emotion as it 'happens' is the key to your EI. Developing self-awareness requires tuning in to your true feelings. If you evaluate your emotions, you can manage them.

**The major elements of self-awareness are:**

- Emotional awareness. Your ability to recognise your own emotions and their effects

- Self-confidence. Sureness about your self-worth and capabilities

**2. Self-regulation.** You often have little control over when you experience emotions. You can, however, have some say in how long an emotion will last, by using a few techniques, to alleviate negative emotions such as anger, sadness, or fear. A few of these techniques include reframing a situation in a more positive light, taking a long walk, practising meditation, or doing some relaxation techniques/activities.

**Self-regulation involves:**

- Self-control. Managing disruptive impulses

- Trustworthiness. Maintaining standards of honesty and integrity

- Conscientiousness. Taking responsibility for your own performance

- Adaptability. Handling changes with flexibility

- Innovation. Being open to new ideas

**3. Motivation.** To motivate yourself for any achievement requires clear goals and a positive attitude. Although you may have a predisposition to either a positive or a negative attitude, you can, with effort and practice, learn to think more positively. If you catch negative thoughts as they occur, you can reframe them in more positive terms — which will help you achieve your goals.

**Motivation is made up of:**

- Achievement/drive. Your constant striving to improve or to meet a standard of excellence

- Commitment. Aligning with the goals of the group or organisation

- Initiative. Readying yourself to act on opportunities

- Optimism. Pursuing goals persistently despite obstacles and setbacks

**4. Empathy.** The ability to recognise how people feel is important to success in your life and career. The more skilful you are at discerning the feelings behind others' signals, the better you can control the signals you send them.

**An empathetic person excels at:**

- Service orientation. Anticipating, recognising, and meeting clients'/customers' needs

- Developing others. Sensing what others need to progress and bolstering their abilities

- Leveraging diversity. Cultivating opportunities through diverse people

- Political awareness. Reading a group's emotional currents and power relationships

- Understanding others. Discerning the feelings behind the needs and wants of others

**5. Social skills.** The development of good interpersonal skills is tantamount to success in your life and career. In today's always-connected world, everyone has immediate access to technical knowledge. Thus, 'people skills' are even more important now because you must possess a high EQ to better understand, empathise and negotiate with others in a global economy.

**Among the most useful social skills are:**

- Influence. Wielding effective persuasion tactics

- Communication. Sending clear messages

- Leadership. Inspiring and guiding groups and people

- Change catalyst. Initiating or managing change

- Conflict management. Understanding, negotiating, and resolving disagreements

- Building bonds. Nurturing instrumental relationships

- Collaboration and cooperation. Working with others toward shared goals

- Team capabilities. Creating group synergy in pursuing collective goals

---

**"In a very real sense we have two minds, one that thinks and one that feels".**

**Daniel Goleman**
**Emotional Intelligence: Why It Can Matter More Than IQ**

---

**Exercise Six**

## The 9 Questions to Evaluate You EI

So, how high do you think your emotional intelligence is? To find out, Goleman put together a list of 9 questions to help anyone evaluate his or her strengths or limitations.

1.  Are you usually aware of your feelings and why you feel the way you do?

2.  Are you aware of your limitations, as well as your personal strengths?

3.  Can you manage your distressing emotions well -- e.g., recover quickly when you get upset or stressed?

4.  Can you adapt smoothly to changing realities?

5.  Do you keep your focus on your main goals, and know the steps it takes to get there?

6.  Can you usually sense the feelings of the people you interact with and understand their way of seeing things?

7.  Do you have a knack for persuasion and using your influence effectively?

8.  Can you guide a negotiation to a satisfactory agreement, and help settle conflicts?

9.  Do you work well on a team, or prefer to work on your own?

**Time to think, reflect and to record your findings here from the above exercise:**

Q1.

Q2.

Q4.

Q5.

Q6.

Q7.

Q8.

Q9.

## Looking more at the evidence and research around EI:

Did you know that how well you do in your life and career is determined by both your Intelligence Quotient (IQ) and your Emotional Intelligence (EI)? What that means is IQ alone is not enough to determine success; EQ also matters.

In fact, psychologists generally agree that among the ingredients for success, IQ counts for roughly 10% (at best 25%); the rest depends on everything else — including EI.

A study of Harvard graduates in Business, Law, Medicine and Teaching showed a negative or zero correlation between an IQ indicator (entrance exam scores) and subsequent career success.

A recent international study surveyed more than 500 business leaders and asked them what sets great employees apart. The researchers wanted to know why some people are more successful than others at work, and the answers were surprising; leaders chose 'personality' as the leading reason. Notably, 78% of leaders said personality sets great employees apart, more than cultural fit (53%) and even an employee's skills (39%). One thing to note is the qualities that leaders in the study called 'personality', were emotional intelligence skills. And like your personality, you can learn how to change and improve your EI with practice and perseverance.

According to the World Economic Forum's Future of Jobs Report, one the job *skills* that will make a candidate competitive in the job market of the future is *Emotional Intelligence (EI)*. The WEF predicts it will be among the top ten in 2020.

The Carnegie Institute of Technology carried out research that showed that 85% of our financial success was due to skills in "human engineering", personality, and ability to communicate, negotiate, and lead. They found that only 15% was due to technical ability.

**Time to think, reflect and to record your findings here:**

**Exercise Seven**

## Dilemma

There is no correct answer to this question. But in several studies, it caused some significant emotional upheaval in the respondents as judged by CAT scans. Especially if the problem included simulated animated video of the problem.

You are driving down the road in your car on a wild, stormy night, when you pass by a bus stop and you see three people waiting for the bus:

1. An old lady who looks as if she is about to die.

2. An old friend who once saved your life.

3. The perfect partner you have been dreaming about.

Which one would you choose to offer a ride to, knowing that there could only be one passenger in your car?

Think before you continue reading.

You could pick up the old lady, because she is going to die, and thus you should save her first.

Or you could take the old friend because he once saved your life, and this would be the perfect chance to pay him back.

However, you may never be able to find your perfect mate again.

Is the best answer: "I would give the car keys to my old friend and let him take the lady to the hospital? I would then stay behind and wait for the bus with the partner of my dreams."

I wonder what you chose to do!

**Your plan of action:**

1. What have you learned from completing this chapter?

2. What are you going to do next to improve/better yourself?

3. Is what you want to achieve realistic, and within your scope or abilities/capabilities?

4. How would you know if you were successful in achieving it?

"Every beginner possesses a great potential to be an expert in his or her chosen field."

Lailah Gifty Akita,
Think Great: Be Great!

# The 8th C
## is for
# Confidence

**Trust: Belief: Acceptance**

# Confidence

---

"Believe in yourself! Have faith in your abilities!
Without a humble but reasonable confidence in your own
powers you cannot be successful or happy".

Norman Vincent Peale

---

## Aims

The aim of this chapter is for you to have more of an understanding of
what confidence is, how it is formed, and how it impacts you on every
aspect of your life.

## Objectives

The objective is for you to read the chapter and complete the given
exercises to help you recognise what old, outdated, limiting and
unhelping beliefs you are currently holding onto and maintaining your
lack of confidence and self-belief. How? By looking at your current way
of thinking, feeling, and behaving.

**Let us reflect on what you want to achieve from this chapter here:**

# Confidence

The word **Confidence** comes from Latin *Confidentia* – meaning having full trust. Then from late 15th century. Middle English and from the French C*onfident*(e) meaning firmly trusting, bold.

**Confidence** – noun meaning:

1. A feeling of self-assurance arising from an appreciation of one's own abilities or qualities
2. The feeling or belief that one can have faith in or rely on someone or something
3. The state of feeling certain about the truth of something

**Self** – from Old English *Self, Seolf, Sylf* – meaning one's own person, self; own, same

**Exercise One**

**What do you think confidence is?**

Write down 5-10 words or descriptions to describe what you think or believe confidence is below.

# So, what is self-confidence?

I personally think the expression – 'Confidence is an inside job' – sums it up perfectly. Why is that? Because **confidence** is just simply a belief system – a current state of mind that you run and own yourself. So, ultimately it is our own decisions that gives us the self-confidence and self-belief to live a long, happy, and healthy life.

Learning to manage your thinking effectively is the key to confidence. This is thinking based on past and current experiences and beliefs. *It is* not something that can be learned like a set of rules, or from a book, going on a course or passed on through the generations.

So, what exactly is self-confidence? Self-confidence is that quiet inner knowledge that you are capable about yourself and your abilities. It is when you feel sure and self-accepting of yourself, in what you think, feel, and believe in, alongside the way you act and behave in all situations. And this belief comes from deep inside yourself, in order that you can grow, develop, and thrive to become a better version of yourself.

This is achieved by acknowledging and accepting your personal strengths and weaknesses working within your own abilities, your capabilities, and own skill sets and always striving to better yourself. Not in an arrogant or egotistical way, but in a realistic, secure, and positive way.

So, self-confidence isn't about feeling superior to others, but feeling secure in yourself. However, striking a healthy balance between too much, and too little can be challenging. Too much of it, and you can come across as being cocky, arrogant, overconfident and a bit of a know-all. But equally having too little can prevent you from taking risks, seizing opportunities presented to you, and going for things outside of your comfort zone.

So, building up a strong sense of confidence and self-belief takes time, training, knowledge, and practice and self-acceptance.

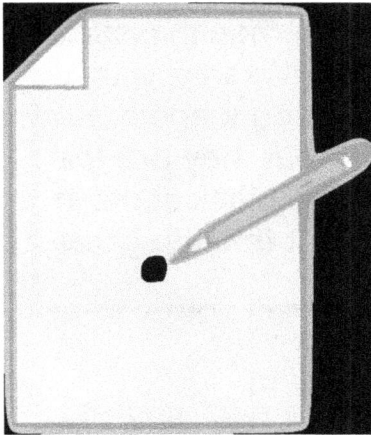

## The question of a blank question paper

One day a professor entered the classroom and asked his students to prepare for a surprise test. They waited anxiously at their desks for the test to begin. The professor handed out the question paper with the text facing down as usual. Once he handed them all out, he asked his students to turn the page and begin.

To everyone's surprise, there were no questions, just a black dot in the center of the page.

The professor seeing the expression on everyone's face, told them the following, "I want you to write what you see there." The confused students got started on the inexplicable task. At the end of the class, the professor took all the answer papers and started reading each one of them aloud in front of all the students. All of them with no exceptions described the black dot, trying to explain its position in the middle of the sheet etc.

After all, had been read, the classroom was silent. The professor began to explain, "I am not going to grade on you this, I just wanted to give you something to think about. No one wrote about the white part of the paper. Everyone focused on the black dot and the same happens in our lives. We have a white paper to observe and enjoy, but we always focus on the dark spots. Our life is a gift given to us by God with love and care. We always have reasons to celebrate, nature renewing itself every day, our friends around us, the job that provides our livelihood, the miracles we see every day."

"However, we insist on focusing only on the dark spots, the health issues that bother us, the lack of money, the complicated relationship with a family member, the disappointment with friends etc. The dark spots are very small compared to everything we have in our lives, but they are the ones that pollute our minds. Take your eyes away from the black spots in your life. Enjoy each one of your blessings, each moment that life gives you. Be happy and live a life positively!"

Author unknown

The moral of the story is life is a bag of good and bad things. We all have positives and negatives along the way. But we must always concentrate greater on the positives for a healthy and happy life. Life goes on no matter what so do not waste your time thinking about the negatives.

Below is your own dark spot exercise, for you to record your own findings.

**X**

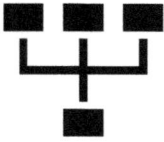

## How do you build up your self-confidence?

The two main contributory factors to self-confidence is:

1. **Self-Efficacy**
2. **Self-Esteem**

**Efficacy** – noun: the ability to produce a desired or intended result

***Self-Efficacy*** is the optimistic self-belief in one's ability or effectiveness in successfully succeeding in a specific situation. Or to accomplish a task, or by producing a favourable outcome.

**Self-Esteem:** The word 'esteem' originally comes from the Latin *Aestimare* which means to: value, rate, weigh, appraise or estimate.

So, if you think about its Latin root, self-esteem is your current estimate of yourself. What you currently think, feel, and believe about yourself as a worthwhile and valuable person.

**Listed below are some of the dictionary definitions of self-esteem**

- Belief in oneself; self-respect
- Confidence in one's own worth or abilities
- Self-respect: confidence in your own merit as an individual person
- A confidence and satisfaction in oneself
- Personal feelings or opinions of oneself
- Pride in oneself; self-respect
- A realistic respect for or favourable impression of oneself
- self-respect
- The holding a good opinion of one's self; self-complacency
- Self-esteem, self-pride (a feeling of pride in yourself)

> **"Nothing builds self-esteem and self-confidence like accomplishment".**
>
> **Thomas Carlyle**

## Here are some beliefs of a person with high self-esteem

- I can comfort myself in healthy ways when I feel sad, angry, or upset
- I can look after my finances and take responsibility for my debt
- I value and manage my own time effectively
- I feel comfortable at expressing my own thoughts, feelings, and emotions
- I am clear about what I will and will not do for others
- I can easily say Yes and No when I want to
- I can easily define and direct myself
- I can set clear boundaries between myself and others
- I can experience joy
- I accept my shortcomings
- I feel comfortable making decisions based on my feelings
- I accept it is OK to make errors, mistakes, and inaccuracies
- I have the right to be perfectly imperfect
- I have a realistic appraisal of myself
- I accept my skills, competencies, and abilities
- I accept full responsibility for my feelings and emotions
- I accept how I feel about myself is not dependant on appearance, wealth, status, or relationships
- I have the right to change, develop and grow
- I feel comfortable saying "I don't know"
- I have the right to be my unique self
- I expect people to be open and honest with me all of the time
- I have the right to change my mind
- I feel comfortable to determine my own priorities
- I believe I have the right not to be responsible for other people's behaviours, actions, or feelings
- I feel comfortable in my own skin
- I feel comfortable following my own standards

**Exercise Two**

## High self-esteem beliefs

Which beliefs of a person with high self-esteem resonated with you the most – and why?

**Time to think, reflect and to record your findings here:**

## The Boasting Traveller

A man who had travelled in foreign lands boasted very much, on returning to his own country, of the many wonderful and heroic feats he had performed in the different places he had visited. Among other things, he said that when he was at Rhodes he had leaped to such a distance that no man of his day could leap anywhere near him as to that, there were in Rhodes many persons who saw him do it and whom he could call as witnesses. One of the bystanders interrupted him, saying: "Now, my good man, if this be all true there is no need of witnesses. Suppose this to be Rhodes, and leap for us."

The moral of the story is he who does a thing well does not need to boast

*From Aesop's Fables*

**Exercise Three**

## Looking to start to develop more mental awareness

Once you know what to be aware of, it's time to start practising.

## Challenge your beliefs

This is the most important step of building up your self-confidence. Once you understand the different types of beliefs you hold, you can start to develop an awareness of them, and then you can start to challenge them.

Challenging old beliefs, ideas, attitudes, and assumptions means looking at new alternative ways of thinking, feeling, and behaving. And the ideal time to challenge old ideas is when you become aware of them.

Why? Because most of us weren't raised knowing that thoughts can be challenged, changed, or got rid of. And if you want to do deep-level, meaningful change, you need to figure out the WHY your mind defaults to the old setting.

## Replace Faulty Beliefs

Actively hunting down faulty beliefs and replacing them takes time and patience. Deal with those negative thoughts and beliefs as they come up. If you want to be an old beliefs expert, think about WHY those negative beliefs came to mind in the first place.

If your beliefs involve other people – as they often will, especially if you're digging deep – it's important to involve them whenever possible. Instead of creating a psychological endeavour and struggling to figure out whether your friend is ignoring you for example, pluck up the courage and just ask.

## Practical Tips

Like anything in life, all of this will be useless if you don't use it. Here are some ways you can actively practice challenging your old, outdated and limiting beliefs right away, in your day to day life.

## The Elastic Band Technique

Wear a rubber band around your wrist, and whenever you have a negative thought, snap it lightly. It's not to hurt yourself, but to use as a gentle physical sensation to raise awareness.

## Mind your language

The language you use creates your reality, which means we are what we think and say.

Have a look at the following statements and what do you notice or recognise?

- Do you really HATE your job?
- Is the food really disgusting, or just not that good?
- Are you really a useless idiot, or did you just make a mistake?
- Are you really that clumsy? Or have you just dropped something?

## Looking for the positives

Is it's a bit unsettling to admit, but whether you see something as positive or negative is a choice! Don't believe me? Try this exercise of listing positives and negatives for a situation or event you feel is clearly one or the other. Most of the time it's a lot more even than you think.

## Give interrogative self-talk a try

Research shows that asking ourselves questions, rather than issuing commands, is a much more effective way to create change. It's as simple as tweaking the way you speak to yourself. When you catch your inner-critic flinging accusations, think to yourself: How can I turn this statement into a question? By asking questions that opens up further exploration into looking for other possibilities and opportunities that could be available to you.

Here are some more examples:

- Am I willing to do what it takes?
- Is it true? What evidence do I have to support it?
- When have I done this before?
- What happened when I did it before?
- What if [insert worst case scenario] happens?
- How can I…?

This type of self-inquiry powers up problem-solving areas of the brain helping you tap into your innate creativity. You're able to greet negative thoughts with curiosity instead of fear.

## Focus on progress, not perfection
To effectively re-frame your thinking, consider who you are *becoming,* and focus all your attention on the progress you are making – the current track or path you're on.

You might re-work your self-talk to sound more like "I am a work in progress, and that's OK." It's pointing you in the direction of positive growth, that is both realistic and achievable. Another example: telling yourself: "Every moment I'm trying to be more conscious about how I am living my life," acknowledges the fact that you are evolving and that you have choice in creating a better future for yourself.

> **"Life is 10% what happens to you
> and 90% how you perceive what happens to you."**

**Time to think, reflect and to record your findings here:**

## Exercise Four

**Listed below are five inspirational quotes around Self-Confidence and Self-Esteem. Which one is your favourite, and why?**

1. "You gain strength, courage, and confidence by every experience in which you really stop to look fear in the face. You are able to say to yourself, 'I lived through this horror. I can take the next thing that comes along',"
Eleanor Roosevelt

2. "The most beautiful thing you can wear is confidence."
Blake Lively

3. "Life is not easy for any of us. But what of that? We must have perseverance and above all confidence in ourselves. We must believe that we are gifted for something and that this thing must be attained".
Marie Curie

4. "Action is a great restorer and builder of confidence. Inaction is not only the result, but the cause, of fear. Perhaps the action you take will be successful; perhaps different action or adjustments will have to follow. But any action is better than no action at all".
Norman Vincent Peale

5. "People who ask confidently get more than those who are hesitant and uncertain. When you've figured out what you want to ask for, do it with certainty, boldness, and confidence. Don't be shy or feel intimidated by the experience. You may face some unexpected criticism but be prepared for it with confidence".
Jack Canfield

**Time to think, reflect and to record your findings here:**

# If
## by Rudyard Kipling

If you can keep your head when all about you
Are losing theirs and blaming it on you;
If you can trust yourself when all men doubt you,
But make allowance for their doubting too:
If you can wait and not be tired by waiting,
Or, being lied about, don't deal in lies,
Or being hated don't give way to hating,
And yet don't look too good, nor talk too wise;

If you can dream - and not make dreams your master;
If you can think - and not make thoughts your aim,
If you can meet with Triumph and Disaster
And treat those two impostors just the same:
If you can bear to hear the truth you've spoken
Twisted by knaves to make a trap for fools,
Or watch the things you gave your life to, broken,
And stoop and build'em up with worn-out tools;

If you can make one heap of all your winnings
And risk it on one turn of pitch-and-toss,
And lose, and start again at your beginnings,
And never breathe a word about your loss:
If you can force your heart and nerve and sinew
To serve your turn long after they are gone,
And so hold on when there is nothing in you
Except the Will which says to them: "Hold on!"

If you can talk with crowds and keep your virtue,
Or walk with Kings - nor lose the common touch,
If neither foes nor loving friends can hurt you,
If all men count with you, but none too much:
If you can fill the unforgiving minute
With sixty seconds' worth of distance run,
Yours is the Earth and everything that's in it,
And - which is more - you'll be a Man, my son!

**Exercise Five**

**The GLAD Exercise** - Training to see the good in life

Every night before you go to bed/sleep over the next 7 days. I would like you to think about 5 small things that you are glad about, or have been grateful for, throughout the day.

And to make this exercise even more powerful, I would like you to record each of the 5 things below, and then . . .

1. Think about each one in turn
2. Visualise each one in turn – by seeing it there in your mind's eye
3. Write each one in turn down in the box below
4. Verbalise each one in turn out aloud
5. Think about how it made you feel in turn – and why

| | ONE | TWO | THREE | FOUR | FIVE |
|---|---|---|---|---|---|
| | Today I have been glad or grateful for … | | | | |
| M | | | | | |
| T | | | | | |
| W | | | | | |
| Th | | | | | |
| F | | | | | |
| SA | | | | | |
| SU | | | | | |

**Time to think, reflect and to record your findings here on the exercise above:**

Monday:

Tuesday:

Wednesday:

Thursday:

Friday:

Saturday:

Sunday:

**Your plan of action:**

1. What have you learned from completing this chapter?

2. What are you going to do next to improve/better yourself?

3. Is what you want to achieve realistic, and within your scope or abilities/capabilities?

4. How would you know if you were successful in achieving it?

> "Confidence doesn't come out of nowhere.
> It's a result of something ... hours and days and weeks
> and years of constant work and dedication".
>
> **Roger Staubach**

# The 9th C
## Is for
# Contemplation

**Thought: Reflection: Planning**

## Time for reflection and action

> **"Don't dwell on what went wrong.**
> **Instead, focus on what to do next.**
> **Spend your energies on moving forward**
> **Toward finding the answer".**
>
> **Denis Waitley**

This chapter is all about you reflecting back on the valuable work you have done so far. And to look at where you are now, to where you want to be, and how you are going to get there. And what steps you need to take to get there.

So, the next question is: 'Is there anything stopping you from taking action, to getting the end result?' If there is, is it: - procrastination, overwhelm, fear of failure or a fear of success, that is stopping you or holding you back from what you want or desire?

**Let us reflect on what you want to achieve from this chapter here:**

## Thoughts

Thought refers to an idea, opinion or an arrangement of ideas produced by the process of thinking, occurring suddenly in the mind.

## Feelings

Feelings are subjective or personal experiences of an emotion or sensation. A feeling is the way that you personally experience something.

## Moods

A mood is your mental state, or state of mind at a particular time. Your moods sum up your thinking and feelings, and it usually lasts longer than a feeling. Moods can also refer to a group or collective feeling, e.g. the country feels depressed, or everyone is fed up of this cold, wet weather etc.

## Emotions

An emotion is an objective way to look at feelings, and the effect it produces by producing those different emotional responses e.g. fear, anger, sadness, excitement, or disappointment etc.

---

"**Negative emotions like loneliness, envy, and guilt have an important role to play in a happy life; they're big, flashing signs that something needs to change**".

**Gretchen Rubin**

---

**Exercise One**

**Belief Systems**

1. What is your understanding of what a belief system is?

2. What old, outdated, limiting, negative or unhelpful beliefs are you still holding onto?

3. How are you going to get rid of those old beliefs of above?

4. What is stopping you from doing it?

5. How different is your life going to be once you have gotten rid of those old beliefs?

**Your plan of action:**

## What wolf are you choosing to feed?

An old Cherokee is teaching his grandson about life. "A fight is going on inside me," he said to the boy. It is a terrible fight and it is between two wolves. One is evil – he is anger, envy, sorrow, regret, greed, arrogance, self-pity, guilt, resentment, inferiority, lies, false pride, superiority, and ego."

He continued, "The other is good – he is joy, peace, love, hope, serenity, humility, kindness, benevolence, empathy, generosity, truth, compassion, and faith.

The same fight is going on inside you – and inside every other person, too."

The grandson thought about it for a minute and then asked his grandfather, "Which wolf will win?"

The old Cherokee simply replied, "The one you feed."

Are there any old, outdated, negative limiting beliefs that you are still feeding?

Are there setbacks in your childhood that still have a hold on to?

Whenever you baulk at a challenge, ask yourself if you are being held back by a limiting belief or assumption, carried over from a bad experience from your childhood or just one unfortunate episode from long ago.

**Exercise Two**

**Thinking**

1. What are your thoughts about thinking?

2. What old, outdated, limiting, negative or unhelpful thoughts do you recognise in yourself?

3. How are you going to change your thoughts?

4. What is stopping you from doing it?

5. How different is your life going to be once you have changed the way you think about things?

# Your plan of action:

## Love and Ego

Once there was an island where all the feelings lived together.

One day there came a storm in the sea and the island was about to drown.

Every feeling was scared but Love made a boat to escape.

All the feelings jumped in the boat except for one feeling.

Love got down to see who it was... it was Ego!

Love tried and tried but Ego didn't move.

Everyone asked Love to leave Ego and come in the boat but Love was meant to Love.

It remained with Ego.

All other feelings were left alive, but Love died because of Ego.

**Think it over . . .**

**Exercise Three**

## Communication

1. What is your understanding of the different types of communication styles?

2. What aspect of communication do you need to work on?

3. How are you going to change it?

4. What is stopping you from doing it?

5. How different is your life going to be once you have changed your communication style?

**Your plan of action:**

# Effective Communication

Jack and Max are walking from religious service.

Jack wonders whether it would be all right to smoke while praying.

Max replies, "Why don't you ask the Priest?"

So, Jack goes up to the Priest and asks, "Priest, may I smoke while I pray?"

But the Priest says, "No, my son, you may not. That's utter disrespect to our religion."

Jack goes back to his friend and tells him what the good Priest told him.

Max says, "I'm not surprised. You asked the wrong question. Let me try."

And so, Max goes up to the Priest and asks, "Priest, may I pray while I smoke?"

To which the Priest eagerly replies, "By all means, my son. By all means."

**Moral: The reply you get depends on the question you ask.**

**Exercise Four**

## Personal sense of power

1. What is your understanding of what the Locus of Control (LOC) is?

2. What aspect of your locus of control do you need to change?

3. How are you going to get change those old beliefs from above?

4. What is stopping you from doing it?

5. How different is your life going to be once you become more Internal?

**Your plan of action:**

**Control Me, Control You, Control Us**

when alone with my thoughts,
I contemplate control
and many other things so mysterious
control what exactly is this puzzling aspect of life?
an illusion, reality, wait, it's only an idea, right?
or something else altogether, like a guiding force
control has no substance, control isn't tangible
yet this thing, I can see, I can hear, I can feel
control is a beautiful thing when we possess it
control is power, control is responsibility
control is an ultimate privilege
If we lose it, we become unbalanced
no longer harmonious, we feel powerless
and behind this large grey cloud
I see a golden outline I know the sun is there
yet sometimes I wonder are we puppets on a string?
and does anyone actually control anything?
control is defined as:
to have power over something
to direct the behaviour of a person or animal
when I try to grasp and hold control,
I find it's a slippery bar of soap
sliding through my fingers


A poem by Sunprincess

https://www.poemhunter.com/poem/control-me-control-you-control-us/ - 27.02.2018

**Exercise Five**

## Personality Types

1. What is your understanding of what a personality type is?

2. What predominate personality type did you recognise in yourself?

3. What aspect of your personality do you need to change?

4. What is stopping you from doing it?

5. How different is your life going to be once you have changed them?

**Your plan of action:**

# Personality

> "There is an amazing power getting to know your inner self and learning how to use it and not fight with the world. If you know what makes you happy, your personality, interests, and capabilities, just use them, and everything else flows beautifully".
>
> Juhi Chawla

**Exercise Six**

**Looking more at your personality in a job, career, or business situation?**

1. What personality type did you recognise in a job, career, or business situation?

2. What old, outdated, limiting, negative or unhelpful beliefs do you need or want to change to get your ideal job, career, or business?

3. How are you going to go about it?

4. What is stopping you from doing it?

5. How different is your life going to be once you changed it?

**Your plan of action:**

## Hercules and the Waggoner

A Waggoner was once driving a heavy load along a very muddy way. At last he came to a part of the road where the wheels sank half-way into the mire, and the more the horses pulled, the deeper sank the wheels. So, the Waggoner threw down his whip, and knelt down and prayed to Hercules the Strong. "O Hercules, help me in this my hour of distress," quoth he. But Hercules appeared to him, and said:
"Tut, man, don't sprawl there. Get up and put your shoulder to the wheel."

The moral of the story is the Gods help them that help themselves.

*From Aesop's Fables*

**Exercise Seven**

## Looking more at your skills, personal and physical attributes?

1. What skills, personal and physical attributes do you recognise in yourself that need to change?

2. How are you going to go about changing it?

3. What is stopping you from doing it?

4. How different is your life going to be once you changed it?

5. Is this true?

**Your plan of action:**

**Those skills, personal and physical attributes that you hold in your hands**

"Long-term, we must begin to build our internal strengths. It isn't just skills like computer technology. It's the old-fashioned basics of self-reliance, self-motivation, self-reinforcement, self-discipline, self-command."

**Steven Pressfield**

**Exercise Eight**

# Looking more at self-confidence and self-esteem?

1. What is your understanding of what is self-confidence and self-esteem?

2. What old, outdated, limiting, negative or unhelpful beliefs do you need or want to change to get more confident?

3. How are you going to go about it?

4. What is stopping you from doing it?

5. How different is your life going to be once you become more confident?

**Your plan of action:**

## The Frog and the Ox

"Oh Father," said a little Frog to the big one sitting by the side of a pool, "I have seen such a terrible monster! It was as big as a mountain, with horns on its head, and a long tail, and it had hoofs divided in two."

"Tush, child, tush," said the old Frog, "that was only Farmer White's Ox. It isn't so big either; he may be a little bit taller than I, but I could easily make myself quite as broad; just you see."

So, he blew himself out, and blew himself out, and blew himself out.

"Was he as big as that?" asked he. "Oh, much bigger than that," said the young Frog.

Again, the old one blew himself out, and asked the young one if the Ox was as big as that. "Bigger, father, bigger," was the reply.

So, the Frog took a deep breath, and blew and blew and blew, and swelled and swelled and swelled.

And then he said: "I'm sure the Ox is not as big as . . . but at this moment he burst.

The moral of the story is self-conceit may lead to self-destruction.

*From Aesop's Fables*

# C is for Completion

## Our journey has now ended

As we have now come to the end of our journey together. I genuinely hope you have enjoyed reading my workbook, doing the exercises, reading the true real-life stories, fables, poems, and inspirational quotes. Just as much as I have enjoyed researching, planning, writing, and putting it all together. To give you the workbook you have just read now.

I would love to hear your thoughts, comments, and feedback on my workbook. So, if you would like to comment, please email me direct at: julieleatherland@gmail.com

Here is my parting quote that reflects the journey you have taken with me. By you taking that very first step towards your journey of self-discovery and learning. And knowing and accepting that this is the first part of your journey through life. With those newly found skills, knowledge and understanding of yourself, and others, that you have learned through this workbook. So, that you can take them forward with you, to live a long, healthy, prosperous, and rewarding life. By finding your own success in which path you choose to take.

With very best wishes

Julie Leatherland

April 2018

To end our journey together, I thought I would end with one of my favourite motivational quotes from Lao Tzu, an ancient Chinese philosopher and writer.

> **"The journey of a thousand miles begins with the first step."**
>
> **Lao Tzu**

So, go ahead and take your very first step to wherever you wish to go, and to do whatever you want to do … as the only thing that is stopping you – is you!

# References

Kelly, R (2011). Rob Kelly - Thrive. Cambridge, England: Rob Kelly Publishing: (Kelly, 2011)


Wentz, F.H (c2012). Soft Skills Training A workbook to develop skills for employment. United States of America: Library of Congress Control Number: 2011963040.In-text citation: (Wentz, c2012)


http://www.aesopfables.com/ 25.03.2018

Source: Henry Woodcock, The Hero of the Humber; or, The History of the Late Mr. John Ellerthorpe, 2nd edition (London: S. W. Partridge, 1880),pg. 32.


http://psych.fullerton.edu/jmearns/rotter.htm


In my book of poetry, Poems from the Edge, I explored these themes. Title of the poem is Who am I? Available from: https://www.christophertitmussblog.org/who-am-i-a-short-reflection-and-poem
Permission to reprint from Christopher Titmuss – February 2018.


Suzanne Read
17th December 2011
By RavenSummerisle, Dec 17, 2011, 2:30:14 AM
Literature/Poetry/Emotional/Urban & Spoken Word
Obtained https://ravensummerisle.deviantart.com/art/The-Job-Application-Poem-274339368 - 23.02.2018


Daniel Goleman, Emotional Intelligence: Why It Can Matter More Than IQ


© Amy
Published: April 2008

Source: https://www.familyfriendpoems.com/poem/communication on 27.02.2018


A poem by Sunprincess
https://www.poemhunter.com/poem/control-me-control-you-control-us/ - 27.02.2018


http://journals.sagepub.com/doi/abs/10.1177/0011000011423553?journalCode=tcpa


https://www.careerkey.org/choose-a-career/hollands-theory-of-career-choice.html#.WrgjvljwaM8